JOY
IN THE
JOURNEY

Walking with Grit and Grace Through Alzheimer's

*May you always find
Joy in your Journey
Nancy Howie
2018*

Nancy Elizabeth Howie

Joy in the Journey
Walking with Grit and Grace Through Alzheimer's
Nancy Elizabeth Howie

© Copyright 2018 Nancy Elizabeth Howie
Copyright ©2018
All rights reserved.

Nancy Elizabeth Howie
Pineville, North Carolina

BookWise Publishing, Riverton, Utah
Bookwisepublishing.com

Library of Congress Control Number: 2018946365

Nancy Elizabeth Howie
Joy in the Journey /Nancy Elizabeth Howie

ISBN 978-1-60645-221-9 Paperback $14.99
ISBN 978-1-60645-222-6 eBook $7.99

10 9 8 7 6 5 4 3 2 1

Printed in the USA
8272018

TABLE OF CONTENTS

DEDICATION

To my beautiful Mother whose long journey home brought to my life the grace of God and the belief that we are given courage, strength, hope, and unconditional love that will carry us through all our days.

To my brother, my Hero of the Faith, whose life taught me forgiveness and redemption and brought to my life love without end.

To my family, who taught me that even though Alzheimer's Disease may bring pain and loss temporarily, it can never destroy the bond of love given to us by our Awesome God.

To my friends, who walked beside me, holding my hands, and being the powerful voice of God and the hands of God in my life both then and now; who gave me the encouragement to write my mother's story—my story—so those who walk, or will walk, this same journey with a loved one in their lifetime may know, that in the end, they will see the gifts their journey has brought to their lives; and they will know they have found peace and joy in the journey.

With gratitude to the Keeper of us all for the *Blessing*!

Every experience, no matter how bad it seems,

holds within it a blessing of some kind.

The goal is to find it.

—BUDDHA

Prologue

It's morning at Meadow Brook Nursing Home. During the last ten months, this has been my mother's abode. Most days, I feel it is mine, too. Life, as I have known it, is a blur. Alzheimer's has taken Mother from herself, her family, and her friends. It has demanded a grit and grace in our everyday lives beyond human comprehension.

"I am tormented! Help me! Take this torment away! Help me! Help me! Help me," she screams.

Daily I have fought to do that, to bring peace to her life. With every utterance, my heart is torn apart, and I cry out to God to not forsake us in our fight. This disease has taken us from the heights of Heaven to the pits of Hell. Today is different. After my second 36-hour shift at Meadow Brook this week, sleep comes in moments for me or not at all, causing me to be exhausted within and without.

Hallway lights outside Room 2128 announce the arrival of the first shift. The quiet peace of the night will soon be replaced with the bustle and activity of a new day, a scene to which I have become accustomed over the past few weeks

1

is now the routine of my daily life. I am sitting at Mother's bedside, holding her hand.

After her visit from the "Old Folks' Friend" three weeks ago, the death watch began. Meadow Brook has become the "Valley of the Shadow." For a few moments here and there, Mother awakens. Her mind is clear. God has given me the greatest gift of all: He has given me my mother back. We hold tight to each other. We sing. We recite poems from her childhood. We talk about her life and her death.

She slips in and out of consciousness. My mind races through the pages of our lives and reviews all the experiences that have brought us growth, both through gain and through loss. Her frail body is fighting to stay, but she will not win this fight. It is her final chapter; her time to go.

Looking in her face, I see a glowing, radiant, child-like spirit filled with love. As I hold her hand, I think of all the hands she has held and comforted in her lifetime. I know that I must tell her story—which ultimately is my story, too—with the hope that it may bring a degree of peace to the hearts of those who have walked, or will walk, the same road. This is our story—the chronicle of the life of a beautiful lady and her family—a life humbly begun, now ending with the devastation of Alzheimer's.

Mary Ann Howie, my mother, has lived a long and fruitful life filled with devotion to the noblest causes, ones which evoke human loyalty and commitment. She has lived for her faith, her family, and her friends. She has been deemed by many the last of the great Southern Ladies whose gentle ways have been portrayed in graciousness throughout her entire life. She has lived with abundant vitality and in quiet solitude.

She has loved people, places, and things—places as humble as her home and as grand as those visited through her travels. The things she has loved, she accumulated through hard work and endowed with memorable stories, making them more than just things. They vividly evoke times and experiences we have shared. This journey had imbued Mother with simple elegance, beauty, and meaning in life. God has used her as an instrument in His hand and filled her with His voice, allowing her to give to others the greatest gift given to mankind—unconditional love.

Come with us and experience our joy in her journey home.

—Nancy Elizabeth Howie

Carolina Blue Sky Days

Small-Town America, 1913

On February 17ᵀᴴ, the heavens opened right in front of the fireplace on North Davidson Street and welcomed a baby girl to the sleepy southern town of Charlotte, North Carolina. Most children were born at home in front of the fireplace while Father walked to get the doctor. The next to last of five children, my mother, Mary Ann, was beautiful, with cherub lips and blue eyes that sparkled with delight, a temperament that would be a part of her forever. Her parents chose her name before her birth. It's meaning—girl full of faith, love, and patience—seemed to describe their soon to be bundle of joy. Little did they know at the time that this definition of Mother's name would be engraved in her heart from the moment she was born and would follow her all the days of her life!

Mother's father, Robert E. Lee Russell, worked in the local lumberyard. Mother's mother, Dora Candace Russell, was a "stay-at-home-mom." The Russell home was modest, but adequate for their family. It was made of old brown wood siding, had a large front porch, an outhouse in the back, and a yard large enough for a few chickens, a cow, two apple trees, and a garden to grow fresh vegetables.

A new home that size, and their home was not new, in 1913 would cost an average of $4000 and was affordable if you made the average annual income of a working man, around $1300. A new car could be had for $500, and gas to fuel it was twelve cents a gallon. If you craved a bologna sandwich, a loaf of bread was six cents. Washing down that sandwich with milk, if you could drink a gallon, was thirty-six cents.

President Woodrow Wilson and his VP, Thomas Marshall, were competent. The state of the U.S. economy had gold holding at $20.67 an ounce and silver at fifty-four cents. The DOW held at about 78.

The Geiger counter made its appearance and was an ominous portent of things to come. The average life expectancy was fifty years; other than this sad fact, it was mostly a good time to be alive.

Families tended to be large, with strong bonds. The Russells would gather around the fire in the evenings or, if the weather was temperate, on their front porch, and talk. There was no radio or television to impede their conversation. Neighbors knew each other by name and naturally took care of each other, sharing vegetables from gardens, an extra apple pie, and helping an already busy mother with a new, bustling baby girl.

Mother was destined to attend the neighborhood school and church, mostly Baptist ones in their little town. Since transportation often consisted of your own two feet, a small town was intimate, neighborly, affectionate, and close. Nurtured by everyone, many of those neighbors remained a vital part of Mother's world her entire life.

More fortunate residents had accouterments like indoor plumbing, but those without it didn't know the difference. The outhouse served its purpose well. Some folks had an icebox or lived near someone who did. Many households owned one cow, a half dozen chickens, and worked a productive garden, which supplied most of the food at meal times. Mother was milking the cow at six. It was a few more years before she was given the task of ringing a chicken's neck. This was an honored responsibility for children to acquire. Mother knew if she allowed the chicken to run away, it might end up becoming the main course on a neighbor's Sunday dinner plate. Mother took this newly acquired responsibility seriously!

Small Town America didn't know the meaning of locks on doors or screens on windows. Neighbors treated each other with respect, and that respect included possessions as well. That's not to say there weren't some bad seeds amongst the good—but that was the exception—not the rule.

Reading by the light of the fireplace or an oil lamp was the standard, and the book was generally the Bible. My mother's mother made her clothes and hand-me-downs were worn until they literally wore out. Clothes had no labels, except the invisible one, "Made by Mama." A washboard was harsh, as was lye soap, so natural fibers broke down more easily, hastening the end of the garment; but fresh air was the dryer, and that made up for myriad laundering faults. The smell of clothes dried in the warm southern sun was heavenly.

Back to natural fibers; most apparel was cotton and everything had to be pressed with a flat iron heated in the fire. Bricks from that same fire warmed the bed at night, with a hand-sewn quilt or two and other warm bodies to share the space.

The street in front of the house was the first choice when playing games like baseball, but most games were made-up. Front or backyards were shaded by large deciduous trees, perfect for tree houses. Agility seemed to be inborn for most of the neighborhood kids, with only an occasional broken arm caused by falls from the heights.

It was a common practice for children to memorize poems and recite them for family and friends at home, church, and school. Respect for elders was ingrained, and childhood friendships lasted lifetimes. Families thrived on responsibility. No one existed unto themselves. It took all working together to make a house a home. Good values were taught by example and were the norm of that time.

Those born in that Small-Town America were the last of the truly gentle people. Mother was that and more. Those gentle ways sustained her and added depth to her life, guiding her destiny.

Sunrise, Sunset

Life is a series of growing experiences

encompassing both tragedy and triumph.

Each one leaves its mark on our lives.

We are who we are based on

how we are affected by each experience.

The Growing Years, 1926 to 1971

MOTHER WAS THIRTEEN WHEN HER MOTHER DIED. I remember her saying . . .

"Mama had not felt good for several days. She seemed so tired, which was not like her at all.

"As we children were leaving for school that morning, she called us all to her bedside—one by one. The message she shared was full of the love she felt for us, tempered gently with a commission of responsibility to always take care of each other. And off to school we went.

"Mid-morning, the principal called me to his office. Mama was sick, and I was to go home immediately. I ran all the way but arrived too late. She died while I was running. In those days, the cause of death was usually listed as *natural*, but we always believed it was her heart. I liked to believe that her heart was so full of love that it just exploded. That was the way Mama was."

Soft as the voice of an angel,

Breathing a lesson unheard,

Hope with a gentle persuasion

Whispers her comforting word.

Wait till the darkness is over.

Wait till the tempest is done.

Hope for the sunshine tomorrow,

After the shower is gone.

"*Whispering Hope* was the song sung at Mama's funeral. The words filled my young heart and gave me hope. She always found the sunshine amid every storm—and so would I."

With the re-marriage of her father shortly after that, Mother found herself in a very unpleasant situation. Her new stepmother brought her two girls into the Russell family, and they became the favored children. Her father became an alcoholic, and Mother, her sisters, and brother were treated very badly as stepchildren. She and her younger sister, Georgia, went to live with an older sister, Eva, and her husband, Erwin, to escape. Life was not easy for them.

To make ends meet, Mother dropped out of school and went to work. Growing, always changing to meet life head on, that was my mother. She later returned to school and completed her high school courses. Returning was destiny, for, upon her return, she met Jimmy Howie.

Mother always called herself the ugly duckling and felt that Georgia, her youngest sister, was the beautiful swan. Since this was her self-perception, it seemed, at the time, that Jimmy saw her that way as well. But Jimmy fooled everyone. He saw my mother as his beautiful swan.

In November 1934, they were married at the preacher's home. They honeymooned in Greensboro, North Carolina at the King Cotton Hotel. That was the first of many ventures outside their small town. Upon returning to Charlotte, Jimmy became the manager for the A&P grocery store and Mother took a job with the Dupont Corporation.

They lived in a duplex on East Fifth Street. In the coming years, they bought their first home on Belvedere Avenue. Mother loved to garden, and their yard was a showcase of flowers. She believed that the beauty of the garden was God's gift to each of us—that His beauty was seen in each petal of every flower. The iris was her favorite, and she had over fifty varieties planted there.

Mother only lived in two more houses in her life, but she always took some of her iris with her. To this day there are still some of her original bulbs in the yard of her last home. These years were kind to the young Howies. They grew with each other, traveled together, played together, prayed together, and worked together as they had been taught to. Jimmy soon opened his own grocery store: Howie Food Store on the corner of 7th Street and McDowell near uptown Charlotte.

Mother continued to work, but they wanted children desperately. They tried and tried, but were unsuccessful in conceiving. In 1946, they adopted my brother, John. No words could be adequate to describe the joy they felt April 17, 1946, when they brought John home. It was on this day that Jimmy became Daddy.

When Mother and Daddy adopted John, they told Mrs. Workman at the Department of Public Welfare, who was instrumental in placing their baby boy, that they wanted a daughter in two years. And, in 1948, that wish was granted. They adopted me, Nancy Elizabeth, on March 22, 1948. Their family was complete! The first few weeks of their lives as new parents of two were rocky, to say the least. I cried and screamed for hours at a time. I did not want to be held or coddled. Mother tried everything she knew how to do to calm me, but nothing worked. She talked to Daddy and told him that something was just not right. No matter what she tried, I was not forming a bond with her. She suggested that they call Mrs. Workman and take me back as it was just not working out. Daddy told her if they took me back, that they would not get another child. God bless my daddy!

Mother called Dr. Johnston and took me in for an examination. Turns out my ear drum had burst, and after treatment for this, I completely fell into the arms of my mother with no problems.

She had special stories for John and me—the stories of our adoptions—which she told often as bedtime stories. Each was similar, yet different. John's story was full of the scent of a cherry pie baking in the oven when he was brought home. My story was full of the scent of an apple pie being baked in the oven. These pies were served on "John Day" and on "Nancy Day" as part of a Celebration Dinner each year. The love felt in those stories went back to gentler times and to the seed of love planted years before in Mother's heart by her Mama. She called John and me "God's greatest gifts" to her and to Daddy. Mother, Daddy, John, and I grew together, knowing only happiness every day.

In 1951, Mother's father had to be placed in a nursing home. I remember her saying, "It was not easy to take Daddy to the nursing home. It is something you hope you never must do. But the time had come. He was sick, and with everyone in the family working, there was no one to care for him at home. But it seemed even at the nursing home, everyone was too busy to care for him. So, it became my responsibility. I accepted this even though I didn't understand it. He was Father to me, but the responsibility for his care went to one. I guess that is the way it sometimes is. Because of my deep love for him, I accepted his care as an honorable trust and tried to make his last days as comfortable as possible. It was not easy, but you do what you must do—and move on.

"I never regretted a minute of it. I look back and am grateful I had the time to share those days with my daddy. He needed me, and I needed him. Out of the love he gave me all my life, I could give my love to him at the time he needed it most. I remember some of Daddy's last words to me."

He said, "Mary Ann, you are so much like your Mama— always loving and always giving to others—I trust God and pray that throughout your life you always remain so."

Grandpa died in 1951, and my mother lived his last words every day of her own life. At the same time as her father's death, my daddy became ill. He spent nine weeks in the hospital with endocarditis. The doctors did not expect him to pull through. It was during the sixth week that Mother approached Daddy's doctor, Dr. Johnston, to request that she be allowed to take John and me to see him. Dr. Johnston was able to obtain that permission from Presbyterian Hospital, and the date for the visit was arranged. We were so excited to be going to see our Daddy! Upon arriving at Daddy's room, we ran to his bedside and climbed up in the bed with him. We hugged each other so tightly. A vivid memory of that visit still lives in my heart.

I remember Daddy giving John and me a wrapped sugar cube and one of those plastic puzzles with moving pieces to take home with us. It was a wonderful day for our family. In the next three weeks, Jimmy defied all odds and became the first patient successfully treated in North Carolina with massive doses of penicillin to survive endocarditis. He was transported home by ambulance.

That day is so clear in my mind, as though it was only yesterday. When the ambulance pulled into the driveway, I stood on the front porch while the attendants brought Daddy into our house on a stretcher. They rolled him to his bedroom and put him in his bed. I went and found his hairbrush, climbed up in bed with him and brushed his hair. I lay down beside him, and we both fell asleep lovingly in each other's arms. From that day forward, life changed dramatically for our family, but with the help of Mother, John's and my love, and the care of good doctors, Daddy adapted to his new lifestyle and lived seventeen more years.

Following Daddy's illness, Mother had to give up her job with Dupont and take over the family grocery business. She dove in headfirst and took the bull by the horns. She had known hardship and pain and had the strength and fortitude to overcome any obstacle, shaking inside, but a rock on the outside. Her version of how to handle obstacles such as this was to stick your chin out and smile. That way no one would know the pain you felt, and then go on with life and make the best of every situation.

She could always be heard singing. Later in life, she told me, "When I feel afraid or sad, when my heart is trembling, and I do not know which way to turn, I sing. It is God's way of bringing joy to my heart." That inner joy she felt gave her peace. Mother's attitude gave us and everyone around us the courage to survive any day.

We attended schools nearby. Our family changed churches so we could attend a neighborhood church. These and other practices cemented our place in the community, and our neighbors were a large part of our lives.

Howie Food Store was a family effort, and we all worked together. John and I were taught the grocery store business at quite a young age. We helped stock the shelves, shucked bushels of corn, learned the art of cutting many different types of meat, learned how to make homemade sausage and to grind beef for hamburger, learned to weigh and measure food for customers, learned to operate the adding machine and the cash register, and how to wait on customers. The basic rule Mother and Daddy taught us at the store was that the customer was always right. Daddy stressed being kind and caring for everyone as if they were one of our family.

After breakfast each morning, we shared a devotional from one of Mother's favorite books, *Streams in The Desert* or *Streams in the Valley*. This was a special time of growing that we did not fully appreciate until much later in life. By some standards, we were probably seen as poor, but the richness of the love we felt as a family proved sufficient for our every need.

That is not to say we had a perfect life. As children, we argued and fought like everyone. We'd be angry with our parents for all the typical reasons, but we were taught never to go to bed angry. And, to my knowledge, we never did. A memory that lives in my heart to this day speaks strongly to that valuable lesson. One evening while leaving the family grocery store, I wanted to carry the bag with the angel food cake on top. Daddy told me he needed John to carry it so the cake would not get mashed. I was so angry at Daddy. Mother and I rode home in one car and Daddy and John in another. I did not speak a word all the way home. Daddy and John pulled into the driveway first followed by Mother and me. When the car was stopped, I slammed my hand down on the car seat and said, "I am so mad at Daddy. I don't like him right now, but, I do still love him." That valuable lesson carried through all of our lives was a blueprint to live by.

There were times John and I would have rather been at home playing with our friends than helping at the grocery and at home, but that was not an option. The store depended on each of us pulling our weight and helping. Daddy was home and could only work part-time each day. And it took all of us doing our work at home to keep our heads above water. We accepted this by helping to cook, clean, rake leaves and clean our yard, and by providing for each other just as it had been for Mother and Daddy growing up.

John and I were given the gift of a small-town childhood even during Daddy's illness—and later in life, as our small town grew and values changed, we came to appreciate that as a gift of love.

During those years, Mother loved to entertain. She always had the family for Christmas, birthdays, and many other special occasions. Ours was the gathering place for all. She often commented to me later in life, "For some reason, the responsibility fell to me to keep our family close and together. That was important to me. No meal was too big or too small.

The closeness we felt during those times was reward enough for the effort. Besides, having company gave me a good reason to spring clean the house at other times than in the spring. Having my family together for all occasions was one of the most important parts of my life.

She was an elegant entertainer. She always brought out the fine china, crystal, and silver for these events. There was always a pressed tablecloth on the table, even for our childhood birthdays with just our immediate family. She believed in giving simple refinement to all throughout her life.

Mother and Daddy were part of a Bridge Club with four couples from our church. These participating couples came and went through the years. The nights they came to our house were special. I remember them vividly and was always so proud to be able to serve our guests. The Bridge Club members were family and part of the 'gentle people'. They gave their love to our family for many years.

In May of 1968, at the age of 56, Daddy was hospitalized. He died June 24th. He lived to see John and Nancy grow up and to see John graduate from college. He lived to see our house paid for and knew in his heart that Mother could finish the race before her. Mother's courage and strength enabled her to live through this with all the grace and wonder she had felt from the gifts she had been given throughout Daddy's life. Daddy knew that John and I had been taught responsibility and would be a source of comfort to her, and he knew that we would always be there for her and for each other. By example,

that was the way we had been taught—the small-town way—
how love would bind people together as family. Our many
friends at church and in the community ministered so
beautifully to us. The 'gentle people' just had a way of doing
that.

Daddy's estate only had $17,000 between the insurance
and the sale of the grocery. Mother invested this and never
touched a penny of it. She kept his wallet with his last $17
in it. That wallet and the $17 remained in a drawer of an
old chest untouched for many years. It later was passed on
to Will with the last $15 Mother had in her wallet when she
died. I told Will when I gave him his grandfather's wallet that
he was to keep it with "his inheritance intact." The only way
the money was to be spent was if one day he found himself
destitute. Otherwise, it was to be passed down to his son.

Mother began to make her way in her new life.

The first several weeks after Daddy's death were full of
people helping us. Someone was always at our house, even
if just to show their concern and love. We would sit on the
front porch as bygone days and talk about him and the good
husband, father, and friend he had been to all. That is, all
except John. I guess Daddy's death was hardest on him. He
withdrew into himself and didn't want to talk about him. For
many years, he was not able to be open with his family.

John went to Seminary in Louisville the following fall. I went back to college at Appalachian State to try and complete my teaching degree. I didn't want to go, but Mother insisted. I felt she needed me at home, but as strong mothers do, she continued to insist that I go back to school and she would be okay.

She told me later, "When I came home in the evenings, I would cry myself to sleep. That is the way I dealt with my grief—only my own pillow wet from my tears knew the truth, and, of course, God. I prayed for strength for the day and for the night and found that it was there, for, you see, as time goes by, most people forget about how alone others feel after a death. They go back to their everyday lives. I loved every phone call from John and from you. Your visits were grand. You were both my life, and I would do everything in my power to help you through your lives."

And she did.

Mother later told me that every anniversary of Jimmy's death until her own death in March 1975, that her sister, Eva, would call and ask her to go to dinner with her. Eva always remembered the day and the time (7 p.m. in the evening) that Daddy died and made sure that she was not alone on any of those days. Mother hated to eat alone. Eating was supposed to be a time for family, but she put a smile on her face, got up each morning, went to work, and continued to try and find new joy in her journey without Jimmy.

Mother dealt with life at home with strength and courage. She sold the family grocery in November 1968. Urban renewal had taken the neighborhood, and she knew she could not continue to operate it. She then set about to find employment. She was fifty-five at the time. Finding a job at that age was not easy, but she was persistent and in January went to work at LaPoint Chevrolet as a bookkeeper.

Looking back, I marvel at her resiliency. Mourning the death of Daddy would have been more than enough, but she felt the keen responsibility given her as a child and knew she must give it to us so we could survive on our own in the future. With John in Seminary and me a junior in college, nothing was going to stand in the way of her helping us complete our education. That was important. Mother wanted us to have something she was not able to have—something no one could ever take away from us—the ability to stand on our own two feet and be self-sufficient.

THE MORNING DEW

1971 to 1992

THE YEARS THAT FOLLOWED WERE FRESH AS THE MORNING DEW. The droplets clung to Mother and me and gave us renewed visions in our lives. At every turn, we found ourselves refreshed and revitalized by the events in our lives. John graduated from the Seminary in May 1971.

I graduated from Appalachian State University in June. What triumphs for us all! Mother was the proudest mom at both graduations! She was so proud of our accomplishments she later told me, "Those were two of the most beautiful days of my life. There were times that I wondered if you both would be able to finish school. Financially it seemed impossible—but you both worked and helped me. God is so good to us—His blessings in our lives cannot be counted. We have each other and will always be here for each other. You have made me proud, and I know somehow your Daddy knows and feels the same for the wonderful young man and young woman you have turned out to be. You have chosen serving professions and will be able to give to others the gifts that God has given to you. A mother's heart sometimes overflows. My gratitude is to God for the wonderful children He gave your Daddy and me, and for all you share with me."

John stayed in Louisville for a while. I came back to Charlotte and took a teaching job with the County. I lived at home with Mother for a couple of months and then struck out on my own to sow some wild oats. She missed me living at home with her but realized I needed to be independent. She never went to my apartment unless she called first. She wanted me to have my own life—to feel free to be myself—and to accept responsibility for my life and my actions. That was the way Mother felt she could give me the same courage she had known throughout her life. I always respected her for this.

In July 1971, Mother and I both received a call from John. He was announcing his engagement to Carolyn. The next few months flew by with wedding preparations. The wedding was held at their neighborhood church in November 1971. It was a grand evening for Mother. She looked so beautiful in her formal gown. And she was so proud of John! She always believed in the adage that when your son marries, you do not lose him, but rather you gain another daughter. Mother tried to be a good mother-in-law. She did not meddle in John and Carolyn's business—although there were times they probably felt that she did. Mother let them grow together in their new life. They moved to Fredericksburg, Virginia and settled into their new life together. They called periodically.

I stayed in Charlotte—moved from apartment to home to apartment to home to apartment—growing with each move. I dated and lost in love more times than I cared to count— but always felt I came out ahead. Mother continued to work. I would meet her at church most Sundays. We shared times together, but mostly our lives were lived separately—as they should have been. Mother was simply grateful I was in Charlotte. She enjoyed our times together—and continued to let me be free in my own life.

During this time, Mother went in for her annual physical. She had been noticing a swelling near her neck—especially when she felt she was under stress. The doctor sent her immediately to a specialist who diagnosed an aneurysm. He wanted her to go into the hospital the next day. But, not Mother, as I was leaving for Nassau the next day. She called me that evening and came by my apartment. We went to dinner that night. I asked her how her physical went, and she said that everything was okay. We enjoyed a wonderful dinner and talked mostly about my vacation. I left the following morning for the Bahamas.

The next Sunday evening when I returned, Mother telephoned and asked if she could come over to my apartment She came by and told me of the aneurysm the doctor had found when she had her physical and was going into the hospital the next morning to have surgery.

I was in a state of shock! I asked her why she had waited to tell me. Her words were: "I did not want to upset your vacation. I knew you had looked forward to going and if I told you, you would have not gone." That was the way Mother was—unselfish in all of life. The surgery was scheduled for Tuesday morning. She and I telephoned John to let him know. Carolyn was very pregnant and there no way that they could come. I stayed at Mother's house that night, and we went to the hospital early that Tuesday morning.

Fifteen minutes before they were to take Mother into surgery, John walked into the room. Mother's face lit up. It was as though God himself had walked into the room. Her love for John was so deep, and his sacrifice in coming to be with her filled her heart with love and her eyes with tears. I, too, was glad to have him home. The surgery went well. Mother went home. I went back home with her to stay for a couple of weeks. John went back to Fredericksburg. Everyone fulfilled their responsibility and life went on.

Mother's life and mine changed on May 20, 1971. John and Carolyn's son, Will, was born. He was a beautiful, perfect baby boy! There was gas rationing at the time, but nothing would keep Mother from going to see her first grandson! Three weeks after his birth, we loaded my car and headed to Fredericksburg. We stopped in Greensboro—waited in line an hour and a half—and filled a gas can with gas to ensure we would make it to Fredericksburg. When we arrived, and Mother held her grandson for the first time, it was as though the angels sang in her heart. A picture of that occasion was made for posterity, but even if it had not been, it would live on in our hearts forever. What a wonderful moment for Mother! She had always loved children and had such a special touch with them. Now she had a grandson to love and to nurture. And yes, yet another opportunity to pass on some of the gentle ways—another opportunity to make a difference in yet another life. She could not stop smiling!

As life went on, moment to moment, day by day, Mother and I lived a pretty charmed life. She had always wanted me to get my Master's Degree. Out of the blue, I decided to go to graduate school. I called Mother one night to say I had made the decision to go. Our conversation began in the typical way with the hellos, how are you, and such. Then my words:

"Mother I have decided to go back to school."

There was silence on the other end of the phone. Rarely did Mother not know what to say. In a few seconds, she asked, "How will you pay for this?" I replied, "Oh, Mother, don't worry. I talked with my banker today, and all is arranged. My tuition will be paid, and a note renewed every ninety days until I finish and can begin working and paying it back."

"But what about your job?" she asked.

I replied, "Oh, I guess I didn't tell you. I quit my job today." Again, there was silence on the telephone.

"How will you live and be able to pay your bills?"

"I really don't know, but I will figure it out."

After all, Mother had taught me that where there is a will, there is a way. And I believed her. Bottom line, I did figure it out. I packed my belongings, gave up my apartment, and headed for Boone, North Carolina. A year later, I graduated my Master's in Special Education. I secured a job with the Charlotte Mecklenburg School System beginning that August.

The strength and teachings of Mother's life had served me well, and now she had yet another dream fulfilled. It had been a hard year for her. She missed my being near and her sister, Eva, died in March. Once again, she felt very much alone. My graduating and coming home in July was a shot in the arm for her. John and Carolyn also returned to Charlotte in this same year. And life was good.

The years from 1971 to 1992 were so full of the zest for life for Mother. She traveled to so many places—to Europe, to Nova Scotia, to Hawaii, to Alaska, to the Canadian Rockies— and took a cruise to South America. She would take weekend trips to New York to see Broadway plays. If someone called and said, "Go," Mother's bags were packed and ready. She went on several short trips with her Happy Times Club and occasionally John would take her on trips with his Senior Group from his church.

Mother's granddaughter, Kelly, was born on January 3, 1977, and her second grandson, Josh, was born on June 10, 1981. When she held her grandchildren, you could see God's love at work. After living in probably ten or more apartments in the city, I once again moved home. I had grown weary of paying rent and through the years had grown. Mother had become my best friend. Oh, Mother would never not be my mother, but being her best friend was great! Together, in the summer of 1983, we decided to do two phenomenal things. We put her house up for sale—the house that she had lived in for thirty-five years—packed the car and headed west. We were gone eight weeks and had the time of our lives. We traveled day to day—choosing each night where we would go the next day. It was thrilling to see so much of the United States, and it was a beautiful experience to have shared with each other. Often looking at the photo album from that trip in later years, we got a warm feeling reliving those memories of a simpler time. We could not see the storm clouds gathering—so they engulfed themselves in the morning dew of our lives.

When Mother and I returned from our trip, we began our search for the perfect house. We probably looked at thirty-five houses during that search. One rainy Saturday, our real estate agent called and said she would pick us up and begin our quest again. The first house we went to was it—although we did not want to admit this to each other until later that day. We saw six houses that day.

When the agent dropped us off at home, and we shut the door to Mother's house, we just stood and looked at each other. I reached up and hugged her and started crying. Mother asked me what was wrong. I told her I felt the first house was the perfect one—that it was the house I wanted to buy—that it was the house I wanted to give to her—but I could not afford it. Mother said that she felt the same way. The next day, our agent came to see us, wrote an offer for that house, advanced me the down payment pending the sale of Mother's house, took the contract to the owner, had it signed, and returned with the good news! So it was that Mother got her dream house. Years before, she had cut a floor plan out of the *Charlotte Observer* of her "dream house." After we moved, I found that clipping in the drawer of an old chest. The floor plan was identical to the house I bought.

Mother and I moved in April of 1984. Other than helping us with two yard sales, John and his family were so busy with their family and church life that they were unable to help us move. So, with physical, mental and emotional fortitude, Mother and I packed up thirty-five years of housekeeping and moved with the help of our lifelong friend, Joyce Deaton. There was so much to be done in our new home—most of it in the yard. Mother was in Heaven. She loved the new home— she loved her new yard—she loved her new neighbors—she was simply in love with life. I had not seen her this happy in years. And I was happy, too.

My friends could not understand why I would want to buy a house and have my mother live with me, but they did not have the kind of relationship with their mothers that I had with mine. Our lives were built on mutual trust, on friendship, and on letting each other lead separate lives. We felt like little kids in a toy store. Each flower we planted, each picture we hung, each piece of furniture we rearranged, each time we cut the grass—everything brought us joy! That was because it was shared. Hard work can even be fun when it is shared with someone you love. Mother and I grew through the joy of living and sharing with each other and with family and friends.

Occasionally, when John and Carolyn needed someone to keep the children, or if Mother and I called and it was convenient, or if they had time to celebrate birthdays, Mother could share with her grandchildren. She would have liked to have shared with them more.

But, John was a minister, and his schedule was hectic. There just was never time. If Mother and I had them over for dinner, they had to eat and run. If Mother and I met them for a meal, they had to eat and run. John would pop in to see us from time to time and spend fifteen to twenty minutes with us, then go—busy, you know. Someone always needed him more than he felt Mother and I did. John and his family's lives had been taken over by the fast-paced world in which they now lived. They were consumed by the "hurry and do it now" syndrome. Occasionally Mother would comment on how she wished she could see John and his family more often, but she realized how busy they were. She felt that John had dedicated his life to God through the Ministry and that was his first priority. Mother often said to me, "I prayed so long for God to give me a son. When God found John for your Daddy and me, I told him that I would give John's life back to Him to mold and shape and that I would not question His will. I cannot question the amount of time that John is able to give to me. He is so good to the people in his church. That is what God meant him to do." I had an extremely hard time with that—partly because I did not believe that God meant John to take a more active role in the lives of his congregation than he did in his Mother's life, and mostly because I knew that it truly hurt Mother to not have more opportunities to share with him and his family. I never felt that John did not love us. I just did not understand why that love seemed to come second to everything else in his life.

Mother and I continued to both work hard—at our jobs and in our home. At the end of the day, we would sit on the porch or by the fireplace in the den and talk with each other—without the blare of the radio or TV. We talked about the important things—life and death, our future together, the possibility of long-term care for Mother, financial decisions that would need to be made if long-term care ever became a necessity for her. With her family history, the likelihood of long-term care being needed was slim to none. No one in her family had lived past the age of seventy-four, and they all died of heart problems. I would jokingly tell her that when the time came for her to have the "Big One," that it would have to be in the summer as I simply would not have time to deal with her death during the school year. We both would laugh heartily at this thought! Nonetheless, Mother would say, "We have to plan. We do not know what the future will hold. I want you to know that if you ever need to place me in a nursing home that it will be all right. I will know that you have exhausted every resource before doing that. How will

I know this? I will know because of the love we share and the feeling that I have that you will always take care of me. I want you to know that this will be a road you will have to walk by yourself. I did with my daddy. John and Carolyn are too busy with their family and their church. God will give you the strength to cross any bridge that He puts before you, and you will be okay."

These conversations were a blessing and a curse to my life later. Mother and I talked with our neighbors, we went to church, we read books, we did needlework, we worked jigsaw puzzles, we shopped, we cooked, we sometimes just rode around looking at the City, we hugged, we laughed, we cried, we had each other and were living in a rainbow world.

"All the world was right."

Mother and I lived our lives in a gentler time, unaffected by the fast-paced changes of the world. And, as we grew together, we formed a bond that seemed to make the angels sing and God chuckle.

Storm Clouds Gather

1992 to 1994

WHEN BEGINNING TO WRITE ABOUT THIS TIME, it can best be described by the opening words of *A Tale of Two Cities.* "It was best of times, it was the worst of times, it was the ages of wisdom, it was the age of foolishness, it was the epoch of belief, it was the epoch of incredulity, it was the season of Light, it was the winter of despair, we had everything before us, we had nothing before us, we were all going directly to Heaven, we were all going direct the other way. . . ."

The years flew by in the blink of an eye. Guess the words of an old song, *Time Waits for No One*, are certainly true. In February 1992, Mother was seventy-nine. While not remarkable to some, it was to Mother and me. Remembering that no one in her family had lived past age seventy-four, and she had experienced an aneurysm and had high blood pressure all her life, it was not only remarkable but to me a miracle. She was not only seventy-nine but was still working. She had a part-time job.

Mother got up each morning and went to work for half a day. She was beginning to show some signs of aging. She was not as quick as she used to be. She forgot little things. But basically, her health and her life remained good. She had developed a blood condition known as thrombocytopenia. In layman's terms, her blood platelets were low. This was not life-threatening. I merely took her to have blood work every two months and monitored her platelet count. It would rise and fall and then remain stable for months at a time. She did realize that she was tiring more easily. I begged her to retire, but she would not. She wanted to continue being productive as long as she could, and being productive to her meant continuing to work.

On Valentine's Day, 1992, as I was preparing to leave for work, Mother said, "Sit down for a minute. I need to talk with you. I have decided I want to retire, and I want to do it today."

I got up and hugged her, and the tears fell softly. "Mother," I said, "I think that is great. Just go in today, and tell them you are taking down your shingle. You don't need to worry about giving notice. After all, you won't be looking for another job, so a reference does not matter. Just do it today. You deserve it!" I was afraid that if she thought about it longer than today, she would change her mind.

When I arrived home from school that afternoon, Mother was sitting in her recliner. I looked at her and asked, "Well?" She looked up and smiled and said, "Yes, I have taken down my shingle."

I was so relieved. Life was not as easy for her now, and I felt like slowing down would help her. And it seemed to. She did needlework, read many books, went out to breakfast and lunch with her friends, continued in the Bridge Club, talked on the telephone, worked puzzles, visited shut-ins, ministered to those in need, remained active in her Senior Citizens Club, remained active in Sunday School and in Church, talked with neighbors, worked in the yard, and generally enjoyed being free of work for the first time in her life. But the subtle changes in her getting older began to show more. She needed more daily reminders to keep her life organized. If I wrote these down for her, she continued being able to follow them and functioned quite well on her own. The first year of retirement was good, and little changed our lives.

During this time, two significant events happened in Mother's life. Her nieces' children, whom she had loved dearly all her life, were getting married—one in September and one in December. The brides-to-be came by our house one day. They talked for a while and then came the question. "Mary Ann, we want to know if you would be our honorary grandmother in our weddings?"

I was sitting across the room from Mother, and my eyes welled up with tears. I knew how much she loved these children. I just did not realize fully what her life had meant to them. I knew she was not going to be able to do all the things she used to do much longer. In my heart, I realized what an honor this was for her.

Mother shed tears on that day. Of course, the answer was, "Yes."

In the months to come, Mother's niece, Peggy, took her shopping and bought her beautiful gowns for the rehearsal dinners and the weddings. We shopped for shoes and the appropriate jewelry for each. I could not go with her to the September wedding in Greensboro. I talked to Peggy, giving her instructions as to the care Mother would need. She would need to be reminded of times, would need to be taken to her motel room, would need help dressing for the wedding, and would need to be reminded to take her medication. In giving this instruction to Peggy, I began to realize how much I was doing for her.

I asked Peggy to subtly walk Mother through the process from beginning to end. She was a very proud person and did not want to admit to anyone that she was not self-sufficient. According to Peggy, Mother came through the weekend with flying colors.

The December wedding was in Charlotte. I helped Mother with all preparations. The night of the wedding, sitting in the church, I felt such gratitude to God for these beautiful people in her life. This was another one of the proudest moments in her life and my life. Being a Christmas wedding, her dress was bright Christmas red. When the music began, and it was time for Mother to process down the aisle, a whispered gasp could be heard in the church. She was absolutely beautiful! She looked like royalty to me. Tears of joy coursed down my cheeks—joy for Mother and this beautiful moment in her life and joy for me just because that was my mother! Several weeks later at home, I took pictures of her in her "wedding" dresses. Each photograph would always be cherished as a memory of the elegant life that she lived.

In the moments of the days and months ahead, time began to come to a standstill in our lives. From this point onward, in Mother's life and in mine, I began to realize that things were going terribly wrong. I noticed more subtle changes in her. She was forgetting more and becoming confused about dates and places. She got lost several times while driving but was finally able to find her way home. She lost her car several times in parking lots but was always able to find it with the help of friendly strangers.

Mother began to call me Georgia many times each day. I was concerned, but not alarmed. After all, she was eighty now and had a right to be confused. I would mention changes that I saw to her doctor every three months when I took her for blood work. The doctor would say, "Oh, she's only getting older. She is okay."

It came time for her to renew her driver's license. I was concerned that she might not be able to pass the test and wondered what I would do if she were not able to renew her license. One morning before leaving for work, I reminded her that her license was up for renewal. I told her that I would stop by the Department of Motor Vehicles on my way home from work and get her a copy of the road signs to study. She asked me to tell her where the DMV was located and that she would go and get it herself. I told her not to worry, that I would get it for her.

After work, I stopped and got a copy of the road signs. Upon arriving home, I handed Mother the booklet. She said, "Thank you, Honey, but I don't need that."

I replied, "Yes, you do. You need to study these for your test."

At this point, Mother left the room for a moment and returned with her pocketbook. She said, "No, Honey, I don't need to study those." She handed me her new license. I could have fallen on the floor!

I thought to myself, "Even I have to review the signs before I take the test every four years." She drove to the Mall (which I was sure she could not find), had taken the test without studying, and passed it. She never ceased to amaze me. In my mind, this was an indication that all the little things that seemed to be slipping in her were just that—little things. Mother was okay. She surely knew who I was. She just confused me with Georgia, her youngest sister, occasionally.

At this point in our journey, my life was full of new friends, and I had fallen in love with my new life! Mother's friends would tell me things that they had noticed regarding her memory and actions. I blew them off to age. After all, I was not seeing these at home. The problem was that I was not home long enough to truly see them. One warm evening a friend of mine, Sandy, was having a party for some folks at her school and she invited me. The party was full of fun and laughter. It was just what the "doctor ordered." I was away from the chaos of home where I was me and having fun!

While at the party, I kept looking across the pool at a handsome man who was sitting there reading. Occasionally when I looked his way, he was looking back at me. The words to a wonderful song came to my mind. *"Some enchanted evening . . . across a crowded room . . . you will see a stranger . . . and somehow you know . . . you know even then . . . that somehow you'll see him again and again!"*

The handsome man, Howard, came over to our table after many of the school crowd left. From the moment we met it was as though we had known each other all of our lives! And from that moment on, for ten months, the words from *Some Enchanted Evening* rang true in my life.

Howard's smile, his laughter, his tenderness brought joy to my journey when I needed it most. We formed a bond with each other and with our new friends, the "Selwyn Avenue Gang," who were so full of life. The laughter and love we shared was extraordinary. Howard, Dave and Donna, Sandy and Tim, Lisa, Jerry, Dan, Rick, Mary Margaret, Ray, Barb, and a host of others filled my life with gladness and brought so much joy back into my life. We filled our lives and hearts with love and adventures. From Holden Beach to Mountain Island Lake, to our local pool hall where we danced more than we attempted to play pool, to cookouts, pool volleyball games, sitting with each other poolside solving all the world's problems, to grand birthday parties, to karaoke nights, and midnight dances where we were held tightly in the arms of those we loved. Yes, for ten months, for a moment in time, all the world was right as we shared in the dance of life and love! All this and much more took me far away from the storm clouds that loomed overhead at home.

Looking back later, two things about this time became apparent. First, I knew deep down that I was running away from the inevitable. Second, the bonding of the love relationship that had been sent to me enabled me to cope with the next two years. Of course, that was looking back.

At the time, I was having the time of my life, and to me, Mother was fine. Little reminder notes I might have to leave her were just a result of her age. Answering the same questions forty-two times a day was just the result of her age. Losing things was just a result of her age. Getting lost was just a result of her age. Isolating herself from her family and friends were just a result of her age and being tired.

When I returned from work in the afternoons, she always seemed fine. Who cared if she called me Georgia. If I went to the beach for a week, Mother would be fine when I came home. The house seemed fine. She seemed fine. It was nothing to be concerned about. She was still driving and keeping busy at home. So, why should I worry? The storm clouds were gathering all around our lives, but the sunshine in my life kept me from truly seeing the approaching storm.

Thunderstorm Warning

1994 to Spring 1995

THE SKY BEGAN TO DARKEN. The warning of an imminent thunderstorm was all around. My life was shattered by two events during the beginning of this. In February, Howard died. He simply suffered a massive heart attack at the hospital while visiting his father—no warning—no goodbyes—here today—gone tomorrow—a life torn apart at the seams. I, along with our closest friends, shared our grief and leaned on each other to try and cope with our loss.

During this time, I ran even further away from the home front. I could not deal with more than one loss at a time. I continued to work hard and play even harder. Most nights, I went out with my friends. On the weekends, I partied hearty with them. I gave little thought to the future. I mightily clung to the hands and hearts of my friends and to the love we shared with each other. We somehow muddled through it all. It would take a long time for our hearts to mend, but with each other, we continued the dance that love had given to our lives.

That summer, my second loss came. My dearest friends, Dave and Donna, who gave me the strength to go on in life, had to leave and go back to Texas. I felt as though the wondrous life I had known was finished—and in a way, it was. I was not sure that it would ever be that good again—for love as deep as theirs was hard to find. A poem I read somewhere years ago said, "Long distance is a rotten idea." It was and still is.

The idea of loss was imprinted on my heart. The thunder roared, lightning strikes could be seen and felt all around us. It was then that the realization of losing my mother hit me. I was at home most of the time and day-to-day saw her slipping away from reality. I didn't know how to explain what was happening. I just knew that it was happening. She would go for short periods of time and appear to be holding her own and then would take a nose dive. No one can tell you what it's like to watch a person you love slowly begin to lose themselves. No one can tell you what it's like to have your mother look you in the eyes and have no idea who you are. They have no control, and neither do you. They cannot change what is happening and neither can you. Helplessness against the forces of nature—a thunderstorm warning and no place to take shelter.

It was at this point that I began to keep a journal. At that time, I guess I was doing it for my own sanity. But, whatever the reason, I was glad I did. For, as the warning became louder and the lightning strikes became more intense, I lost the ability to think clearly. Life no longer was reality-based.

Mother and I were actors on a stage, each with a new part to play. The problem was that there was no script. Day to day, sometimes hour to hour, the curtain would open on a new act, and none of the actors knew what to say or what to do.

November 1994 to February 1995

It is as though a bomb has been dropped. Mother's periods of confusion are becoming a part of our everyday lives—consuming our lives would be a better term. I am no longer me. To Mother, I have become her sister, Georgia. She no longer recognizes our house as our home. She is more and more in the past without being able to grasp the present. She says that she irons, dusts, vacuums, etc. and, in reality, does not do so. When I try to do these things, we have a heated argument. It is easier not to do them than to argue with her.

Mother and I have never argued before. This is a new way of life to me, and I do not understand how to cope with it."

During this time, in an effort to try and understand this brave new world, I had been thrust into, I do remember reading somewhere that the role of a caregiver sneaks in slowly and eventually takes over your world. No truer statement could have been made of my world at this point.

The house is going to hell in a hand-basket, and I'm just letting it. I come home from work and Mother tells me about trips she takes while I am away—it might be uptown to meet her sisters (both of whom died many years ago) for lunch. She is still driving, but I am finding out from friends and relatives that she is getting lost frequently. She goes to the shopping center or to the mall and cannot find her car. She has to call friends to come and help her locate it. I do not know what to do. To take the car away from her would devastate her life. Right now, it's all she has left of freedom. Life at home is becoming a little bit of hell on earth. When I go to work, it is the only place where I know who I am. I keep thinking that things will get better, that Mother will wake up one day and her mind will be clearer. There are times when it appears so, and I guess that is where my hope lies.

We went to the doctor in early November. I told him again about Mother's confusion. 'Could this be the beginning of Alzheimer's?' I ask. "If it is, I need to know. I need to know what to expect and how to plan for tomorrow and the next day. I need to know how to handle day to day living at home and to keep home safe for Mother." The doctor says, "I don't think it is Alzheimer's. Your mother is just getting older, and her thinking is not as clear as it once was." I am successful in this visit in getting Mother a prescription for an anti-depressant medication. She is having a period of weeping for no reason— has been talking about dying—continually says she is going away so as to not be a burden to me. Her platelets are lower this time. I leave thinking that perhaps the platelets are really her problem. If she is hemorrhaging with massive bruises on her arms and legs, what is to say that this is not happening in her brain also? Be this the case, the oxygen flow to her brain is not good and, perhaps, this is why she stays confused. There are a million explanations for her confusion in my mind. It does not matter what the cause of her confusion—it is how to deal with it that I need to know. I am sinking deeper and deeper into a hole I do not know how to climb out of. I am losing a part of myself to a disease I cannot understand nor name. I search for books that will help me know how to deal with life, but cannot find even one. The books I find are all so technical and filled with medical information, but none tell me how to cope with each moment of each day caring for my mother who does not even know who I am!

We go to Carolyn's brother's house for Thanksgiving. Up to this point, I have cared for Mother on my own. I often remember her words, 'You will be the one responsible for my care.' But it is time that I ask for help. Soon after we arrive, I take John out on the front steps. I try to tell him what is happening. The reaction to much of what I tell him about Mother is laughter. He does not seem to be able to believe or accept what I am telling him. After all, he does not see Mother on a regular basis. When he does come to visit, somehow, she pulls herself together and appears to be normal. I explain that the situation is far from funny and I need help. I explain that when I end up in the looney bin, and there is no one to take care of Mother, then it probably will not be so funny to him. We agree on some overnight visitations at his house for her. At least that way, I can get some relief. I tell him about my trip to Texas over the Christmas holiday. I ask him to be responsible for seeing that Mother is taken care of. He promises to do this.

The first two weeks in December are passing by with all the festivities at school. The first week out of school, I go Christmas shopping, come home, and wrap all the presents while Mother watches. She cannot understand fully what is happening. I realize that this will be our last true family Christmas— even though, for me, most of it will be pretense. I cry so much during this time. It is so hard to watch the mother I have known and loved all these years being taken away by something bigger than either

one of us. She compensates well when I am with her.
When she is with other people, I am always there
to fill in the blanks for her. I am there to love her
and help her appear normal to the outside world.
But she knows something is wrong. She just cannot
explain it any more than I can. She has begun to
withdraw from the outside world even more.

We went to church at Thanksgiving and have not
been back since. We did not even go over Christmas.
I do not question. It is easier to go with the flow—
whatever that flow might be. It is in December that
I discover Mother's financial plight. I have never
had a reason to look at her checkbook. She always
kept immaculate records. She wants to write a
check to the church but cannot figure out how to
do it. I ask her if she wants me to do it for her.
I do. I begin to question in my mind the state of
her account when I record that check in her check
register. It looks like a disaster—marked through—
and whiteout everywhere. 'When you get your
next bank statement, Mother, let's go through your
checkbook and make sure it is balanced correctly,' I
say. Mother goes into a tirade. I end up leaving the
room in tears. Again, it is easier to run away than to
face the problem. I find that I spend more time in my
room than I do anywhere else. It is the only retreat
that I have.

And, run away I do. Christmas night when we come home from our family Christmas gathering, I ask Mother to move her car, so I can pull mine all the way up in the driveway so she will have use of her car while I am away. We do this, but when she tries to pull back up in the driveway, her car cuts off and will not start again. At first, I am angry. I am tired. I have packing to do and just want to get the hell out of Dodge. I have had about all I can take of the fantasy world I am forced to live.

The neighbors across the street help us push the car up into the driveway. I come in and call John. I ask him to have his mechanic friend come and tow the car to his shop and have it fixed. I also ask him in a whisper in the other room not to bring the car back. As I go to bed that night, I say a prayer of thanksgiving to God for the guardian angel of broken cars. My worries about Mother driving are taken care of—at least for now.

The game plan is for Mother to spend the week I am gone at John's house—coming home during the day so she will be in a familiar environment. Everything is worked out and I am ready to leave. John picks me up to take me to the airport and assures me all plans are made, and Mother will be okay.

While I am in Texas, I call home every day. It does not matter what time of day or night I call, she is always home. I finally figure out that she is not going to John's house. I am livid. But, there is nothing I can do about it, so I simply check it and determine that if I talk with her and she seems okay, then the house must still be standing. I did leave notes regarding her medication and was sure there was something for her to eat before I left. I just did not count on plans being changed for any reason. Oh well, just the first of many plans to go down the tubes.

My trip is a good one. I have been me for a whole week, living in my reality. It is good to feel whole again. Arriving home, I realize how quickly Mother is taking another downhill slide. The confusion becomes greater. Her bank statement comes, and she does let me try to balance it. I discover that she has written ten checks to the church during December, giving all her income for the month to them. I try to show her what she has done. We end up screaming at each other, something we have never done, and I end up leaving the house and driving around the neighborhood to cool off.

What am I going to do? Back at home, Mother has calmed down, and we agree to let me handle her finances for a while until we have them straightened out. I take her checkbook and keep it in my room from that time forward.

Many times she accuses me of stealing her money, of thinking her stupid, etc., but I keep on doing this for her. I have to. This is the one area of her life which cannot become messed up. The fights are endless, it seems. We always end up hugging and crying with each other, but the emotional drain is great. And through it all, I keep hoping that things will get better. I have no understanding of what truly is happening and what the full impact will be.

March to May 1995

Since January, John and his family have let Mother come and stay at their house twice. The visits begin around 6 p.m. one day, and Mother is brought home the next morning. This is hardly what I had in mind, but at least it gives me some peace. I cannot tell you how wonderful it is to get up in the morning and have my coffee in peace. I cannot tell you how wonderful it is to come home to a quiet house and sleep through the night. I am losing it and know it. Life has lost meaning and has become hell on earth to me. I try to remember the good and think about the glimmers of hope that I occasionally see in Mother, but I am reaching the breaking point. I need help!

The end of March we have a family meeting at our home. We talk with Mother about trying to find a place for her to go and live where she can be safe while I work. She seems open to this. I cry as we talk together with the family. I am having to admit for the first time that I am not able to care for her at home anymore. This is one of the toughest realizations I must accept. I always planned to care for Mother and could see no reason why I would not be able to always do this. But I did not count on the demon I call Alzheimer's descending on us in such a harsh and furious manner. John is going to actively seek a place for her as his job better enables him to take an hour or two here or there during the day and visit places.

Two days later, John comes by the house in the late afternoon. It is a Wednesday. He has found a place, Countryside Manor, which is run by a couple he knows well. He tells us that they will be able to take Mother on Saturday. "This Saturday?" I ask. I cannot believe that it can happen so quickly. A part of me wants to jump up and shout, rejoicing that my hell on earth is ending. But the other part of me, which is a larger part, goes into a panic. I must take Mother to the doctor for a TB test and have an FL2 filled out. I have to get her things together, label everything, pack everything, and be ready to take her Saturday morning. How can I possibly get it all done and work? Well, I simply will have to take two days off.

I call in sick. I actually become sick just thinking about all I have to do and thinking about the end result, which is Mother leaving this house—her home—our home—and going to live somewhere that I have never seen. I ask John to set up an appointment on Friday for me to take Mother to see Countryside Manor. It is not that I do not trust him, I just have to see where I am taking my mother to live. He is to meet us there at the appointed hour. In the interim, I make the doctor's appointment and go shopping to get all the necessary items for her. I label all her belongings. I call her niece, Peggy, to let her know that I must place Mother in an Assisted Living Center. I cry and all I know to ask Peggy is that she and her family not forget about me. Mother and I meet John at Countryside Manor Friday morning.

When we drive up, I am impressed with the outside appearance. There are two houses which comprise the Manor. Mother will be in the one on the left. A circular drive brings us to the front. There is a pretty covered area with chairs at the front. Upon entering the house, there is a small living room to the left with a nice sun porch. A small dining room and kitchen are on the right. There are two hallways—one on the right and one on the left—with three bedrooms on each hallway. Each bedroom is furnished sparsely with two twin beds, a nightstand for each bed, two dressers, and a small closet for each resident. It is neat and clean.

I have my first experience that day with residents living in an Assisted Living Center. The few ladies in the living room do not say a word. They are slumped down in chairs or on the sofa and appear to be drugged. One lady walks aimlessly throughout the house talking to herself. We do not stay very long. We go to the Director's house, which is located on the property, and turn in all of Mother's paperwork. On the drive home, Mother and I are both silent. My thoughts are that I just cannot let her go there. Mother has worked all her life, had a beautifully furnished home, is much more active than the people I saw, and bottom line deserves better than this. Mother never says anything.

Back at home, around five o'clock as I am ironing the last of her clothes and trying to get them labeled, Mother speaks and simply says, "I refuse to go there. I have worked hard all my life. My money is mine. I will not spend it to go to that place to live." At first, I try to reason with her. There is no reasoning. She becomes extremely argumentative. I finally sit down and through tears say, "Mother, I agree with you."

I did not realize at that time the significance of those words. They would mean almost four more months of hell at home for me before there would be no choice. Mother and I both cry and hold each other. God, I do love my mother, and I will do anything to help her. I try to get John on the phone, but he is not to be found. I finally talk to Carolyn and let her know Mother's decision. She gives me the number for Countryside Manor, and I call and talk with the Director.

I thank her for saving the space for Mother and explain the situation. She gives me my first pointers in dealing with the situation in the future. She says it would be best to involve Mother in all decisions regarding her care whether she can fully comprehend them or not. When looking for places in the future, she said to take Mother with me to see them before the decision is made to let her live there. She is very understanding.

Later in the evening, John calls. He is extremely angry with me. "We should just pack her bags and take her out there and leave her," he says. I end up crying and screaming at him—will not let him talk with Mother—and finally hang up on him. The audacity of him to even talk to me like that! He has no clue as to the hell I have experienced every day and no clue as to why any of this is happening. In the first place, we are not leaving Mother anywhere. I will always be a part of her life no matter where she is. She is not excess baggage just to be dropped off somewhere. The anger in me is uncontrollable. I cry so much that day that I cannot sleep that night. John's attitude with me after that day was that "I had a place for Mother, and you let her turn it down."

I stopped asking for respite, and it stopped being given. Amazing how a disease brings out the best and the worst in families. It should be a time to pull together and band together trying to help each other. But most times, it works the other way, and family relationships crumble.

Life at home continues. My daily notes to Mother become longer, and I realize that they are doing no good. Medication is my strongest concern, but I cannot be here to be sure it is being taken, and I truly have gotten to the point that I say, "Oh, well, if Mother does not take her medication and dies, it will not be my fault." And yet, there are still more times than not that I try to reason with her about that and so many other issues. Reasoning is the one thing I need to give up, but it is the only sanity in my world.

I go to the beach during spring break. I really do not feel good about going, but I have to get away. I do not ask John for help. I do let him know that I am going. I let neighbors and other friends know that I am going just in case something happens and I must come home, someone will know where to find me.

I leave on a Saturday. I feel as though a million-pound boulder has been lifted from my shoulders. By Monday night at the beach, I am a wreck. I cannot sleep. My heart starts pounding. I feel as if I am going to have a heart attack. It is so real that I get up and write down my life insurance policy numbers on a card.

The next morning my heart continues to pound. Around 11 am, I confess to my friends what is happening to me. It is decided that I am going to the Emergency Room at the nearest hospital. In the Emergency Room, they hook me up to a monitor, examine me. I talk with the doctor on call. He asks if I have been under any stress lately. I laugh out loud. I explain my home situation to him. After resting there for two hours and taking medication, my heart settles down to a normal pace. What has happened is that I had an extreme anxiety attack. I have been trying so hard to enjoy myself, yet my body would not let me relax and have a good time.

I get a prescription filled and enjoy the rest of my week at the beach. I call home each day, find Mother to be talking out of her head, but at least I know she is at home, and the house has not burned down.

The week after I return from the beach, I go to my doctor. I explain what happened to me at the beach, what I am going through at home, and he immediately puts me on Prozac. Yes, I am depressed to the point of not wanting to go on with life and yet knowing that I have to.

My doctor gives me the best advice yet. He tells me that it is okay to be Mother's sister, Georgia. If Mother calls me Georgia, simply be Georgia. Do not try to reason with her anymore. Reasoning is not possible with a person who has Alzheimer's. That word! There is that word for the first time from someone else—and a doctor at that! I ask him if he truly thinks that Alzheimer's is the problem. He says that there is no doubt in his mind after listening to me explain what is going on with Mother.

He took my hands in his and told me that he knew that the point when Mother lost me as Nancy was so difficult to understand. He explained it to me this way: "Alzheimer's reaches a point where the person with the disease will no longer be able to make any new memories, and for some cruel reason, they often lose the ones closest to them and that their brains simply will not let them remember. Imagine yourself not being able to recognize those closest to you. Imagine yourself stuck in time, never being able to make a new memory. Imagine the frustration and confusion that would take over your world."

I never forgot these words, and they were a blessing in helping me to cope with everyday incidents in a more compassionate way—most of the time. I leave his office saying thank you to God for a doctor who listens and understands. I still do not know what I am going to do for the future, but I now know my suspicions are true. Alzheimer's Disease is real!

Life becomes a little easier. Oh, it is far from a piece of cake, but my fuse stays lit a little longer before going off and does not go off nearly as many times. I have given into the fantasy world my mother is living in. I have become Georgia.

As Georgia, Mother and I work in the yard. Oh, how she still loves to garden. She tires extremely easily, but otherwise seems content to be outside with me—Georgia. I buy flowers, flowers, flowers, flowers, and more flowers. Our yard is absolutely the most beautiful that is has been since we moved to this house. So many times, Mother simply stands in the kitchen window and comments on the beauty. Or, she will go outside and sit under the oak tree and just sit as though she cannot soak up enough beauty.

One afternoon, arriving home from school, I go out to water the plants. While out there, I remember some things I need to pick up for school. When I get back into the house, I ask Mother if she would like to ride with me to Toys 'R Us. She says she would love to go. Mother goes back to put on her make-up. She calls out from her room, "Be sure to go out in the backyard and let Nancy know where we are going so that she will not worry about us."

I walk out the kitchen door and get to the gate to the backyard. I put my hand on the latch to open it. I guess the sound of the latch brought me to my senses. "My God, what are you doing?" I ask myself. "You are Nancy, you fool." That is how consumed I have become living in the fantasy world my Mother's brain has left her in. I am frightened!

Could I slip so far away from reality that I will live in Mother's world with her? I guess that is why I enjoy going to work so much this spring. At least for a few hours, I have my world back as it is supposed to be. I live from day to day and let six weeks pass from the time that placement at Countryside Manor became such a disaster.

One afternoon while talking with Mother, I ask her if I set up some appointments at different retirement homes, would she go with me to see them? It will *just be good to see what is available if we ever need help. Mother agrees to do this with me. I set up four visits for the next week. Those are the only visits we make. Three of the options Mother likes. Two of those three are not financially possible—$1800 to $2500 a month—private pay only. The one that is affordable is an apartment retirement home with no assisted-living areas presently. They are breaking ground for a nursing home, but it will be a few months before it can be completed. One of the options, which is affordable, I will not even consider. It is not clean, and there seems to be chaos throughout. But it is good to go and let Mother be a part of this.*

I decided to get in touch with a care agency that would come to our home and complete an evaluation of Mother and our efforts to cope with her progressive Alzheimer's while attempting to continue caring for her at home.

I talk with Mother many times each week regarding what is happening and the fact that I do not know what the future holds for either one of us. We spend many hours crying. There is just no understanding for us of what we are up against. The only thing I am sure of is that by now, I know we are in it by ourselves. It is up to us to find the help we need, whatever that might be.

No one gives a damn about either one of us. No

one calls to see what is going on. Mother has not been to church since November. Guess it doesn't matter. That is hard for me to accept as active as she has been through the years. You would think that someone would care. I don't go to church anymore, either. I have to stay with Mother. Guess that does not matter, either. Family, church, friends—the losses are only beginning, I fear—for we are now in the midst of the storm.

Amidst the Storm

Summer 1995 to Winter and Spring 1996

THE STORM GATHERS STRENGTH. The winds begin to gust. The rains begin to pelt our lives hourly. There is only uncertainty as to the viciousness of the storm and the destruction that it will render. Questions only bring more questions. There are no answers on the horizon. There seems to be nowhere to turn to retreat from the pathway of the storm. I cry out for help and feel only helplessness.

June to July 1995

School is soon to be out, and for the first time in my twenty-two-year career, I have chosen to teach summer school. The reason being that school is the only place where I am me, where the world is real, where I have freedom. Home is hell on Earth. Home is prison. Home is totally void of reality. And there is nowhere to turn.

In researching retirement/assisted living homes in Charlotte, I come across an advertisement for a care agency which gives help in dealing with problems of aging. I call the listed number and talk with Mrs. Smith, the Director. She agrees to come to our home and do an assessment of Mother and our situation and to offer help with our problems. I feel good knowing this is the first avenue I have pursued which has brought even a glimmer of hope.

I set up Mrs. Smith's visit for June 15th. For the first time in many months, I feel release. Finally, hopefully, help is on the way. As the time nears for Mrs. Smith's visit, Mother seems to be a little better. She continues to have all the same problems but is reacting to me and to life in a gentler way. For brief moments during these days, I become Nancy again to her. Only working half a day with summer school, I don't worry as much having to leave her by herself. I am home by 1:15 p.m. each day.

We meet Mrs. Smith in our home on June 15th. She interviews Mother and me together and separately. We talk about all the issues which are of concern to me. She seems extremely receptive. Mrs. Smith completes an evaluation of Mother and our home and gives us encouragement based on the way she sees us handling our situation. Mother appears so normal while Mrs. Smith is here. It still blows me away that when someone comes to our home, Mother can pull it together for a period of time. I sometimes feel like I may be the one who is losing it. Maybe I am seeing too much and reading too much into the situation. Mrs. Smith leaves and promises to have a report ready for us within the week, which will give us further suggestions and possible residences for us to pursue for Mother.

Four weeks pass. No word from the care agency. I presume this is just another dead end. During these four weeks, Mother has taken another turn for the worse. I cannot leave her except to go to work, and then I alert the neighbors to be on the lookout for her. On Monday, July 10th, she has a doctor's appointment at 2 p.m. I leave her a note letting her know that I will be home by 1 p.m. to take her to the doctor.

I arrive home at 1:05 p.m. to find her gone. Panic cannot describe the feeling I have. I know that Mother is confused to the point of not recognizing her own home. And now, she is nowhere to be found.

I go to my neighbor's home first. They have not seen her all day. I call other neighbors, thinking she became confused and asked them to take her to the doctor. I call our church which is around the corner from our home thinking that maybe she walked over there. She has done that before. Nothing. Within five minutes, our minister, Allen, is at our home. All I can do is pace. I call John's house to see if Mother contacted him, and he is taking her to the doctor. I call the doctor's office to see if she has been there. I explain the situation to the nurse and let her know that if we find Mother, I will call them back. Nothing.

At 1:45 p.m., Allen is standing at the kitchen door. I am pacing the floor in the den. He says, 'Your mother is walking up the street.' I ask him to go and meet her. I am so frightened that I am angry. I am afraid of what I might say to her. Why can she not follow simple written instructions that I leave her? Why must all of this be so difficult? What more can I possibly do? I call the doctor's office to let them know that we have found Mother, and we are on the way to keep her appointment. I meet Allen and Mother in the driveway. Mother says that she rode the bus uptown to meet her sisters for lunch. Her sisters are both deceased and have been for years. There is no reason for me to try and explain this to her. She cannot understand why I am so upset. The red flag of danger just went up at our home. No longer can I leave Mother alone at home to go anywhere.

I will never, ever know where Mother has been. I am glad she made it home safely, but the anger in me continues to take over. We go to the doctor.

I tell him what just happened. He tries to talk to Mother. But, again, he says to me, "She is just aging." We come home, and I try, to no avail, to make Mother understand that it is not safe for her to walk by herself. She only becomes angry and says she is able to take care of herself. If she wants to ride the bus uptown and have lunch with her family, she can, etc., etc., etc. We both end up crying and being angry with each other.

I call the emergency number for the care agency. I explain my plight to an answering machine. Mrs. Smith calls me back around 9 p.m. She promises to come by the school tomorrow and bring me her report. I call the Director of Countryside Manor and also talk to a machine. Where are the people you need when you need them? The Director calls me back at 11 p.m. She wakes me up, but that does not matter. I am in a crisis. Ironically, there is one bed available at Countryside Manor beginning next week. I jump at the chance, feeling like God is finally on my side. I talk with Mother about this the next day. She is too confused to truly understand.

I take Mother to Countryside Manor on Thursday to visit. We talk with the staff and sit in the sunroom for about an hour. I feel like if she shares a part of it with me, then it will be easier for her to accept living there. When we leave, she seems receptive to the idea of coming here for a while. She keeps asking, "If it does not work out, can I come home?" I explain that possibly she could, but we will need to give it enough time to work. I tell her that it is like me going away to college for the first time and being homesick. Rather than coming home, I stuck it out and learned to love being on my own and living with friends. She seems to accept this.

And all the while, Mother seems to slip further and further away from reality. She has begun to tell people that her husband, Jimmy, left her for another woman. She has no clue that our house is our home. I show her our address in the phone book and the church directory. I walk her outside to the street sign. Still no clue of where she is. She simply cannot comprehend and, once again, I am Georgia.

Mother gets up in the morning and thinks that her family is here—lives here—sleeps here. She chastises me for making noise and waking them up. She walks the house looking for them. I play her game and explain to her that they have already left for work. Reasoning with her is out of the question. It is easier to play games and keep the peace as much as possible.

One night I hear her get up. I look at the clock. It is three o'clock in the morning. Fifteen minutes later, her bedroom door opens. I call out to her and ask where she is going. She says that she is going out for a walk. I get up immediately and stop her. All of this is going on in the dark. I tell her she cannot go for a walk without me, and I need to get some sleep to be able to work tomorrow. She says, "Okay, I will just go and sit on the porch." I tell her I would go with her, but that I would rather that she just go back to bed so we may both get some sleep. She finally agrees.

When we get back to her bedroom, I turn on the light so she can see to get back in bed. I almost faint. Mother has on a flannel nightgown, two sweatshirts, toilet paper wrapped around her neck and head, and winter gloves on her hands. I am devastated! I gently help her take off her winter wear and help her back to bed. When she is settled, I go to my room and cry until I can cry no more. My mother is gone, and a person is in her body who I do not recognize and do not know how to deal with. My life as I know it completely falls apart on this night.

So our days and nights continue until Wednesday of the next week. There are no periods of recognition. Mother is on another downhill spiral, and I am an emotional and physical wreck. Allen has ladies from the church stay with Mother Monday through Wednesday while I try to work. It is so difficult to leave her, but so good to be gone from the problem for even a few hours a day. I am in a position of not even being able to go to the grocery store for fear something will happen to her.

Mrs. Smith from the care agency drops her report off to me at school. Obviously, it is a "canned" report. Mother's name is different in many places in the report—replaced by another person's name. Must be nice to make a living ripping off the elderly and their families this way. At least that is the way I see it! I simply file the report away. My mind races during this time. I know that I am going to lose my mother, and I want to keep as much of her as possible with me at home.

Mother has recited poems that she learned in her childhood throughout my life. I realize how quickly she is moving into her world where all of this will be lost. I sit with her one afternoon at my computer. With lots of help, she remembers the poems. I type them into the computer as quickly as we, together, can remember them. Mother cannot understand why I want her to do this. But at this point, it does not matter. I just tell her that I am very emotional and need to be close to her and love her. She accepts this from Georgia.

I take Mother back to Countryside Manor on Wednesday morning. This is the day before she will come to live here. Again, we sit in the sunroom and talk for about an hour. The nurse on duty shows Mother the room she will have. We walk around outside for a while. Then we leave. Mother remains calm about going. I believe the calmness comes from not understanding the full impact of moving.

As we drive away on this day, I have the same feeling of wishing Mother was going to a home more like the one she worked so very hard to have. I wish that there was a way to keep her in her home. But this time it is different. I know that I have no choice. After all, it is clean and neat, and the staff seems nice. And John is friends with the Director. That will surely count for something. In my mind, when pushed against the wall, anything looks better than the circumstances that have forced that push. I just know that I can no longer let Mother stay home. It has become a matter of life and death for her—and for me.

I cry later. I am not prepared for this disease that has taken my mother away from me. I have no understanding of the symptoms. How is it possible for her to stand in front of me, look me in the face, and not know who I am? How can she read daily notes left for her with specifics regarding medication and activities and not follow through with them? How can she get up in the middle of the night in the hot summertime and dress in ridiculous winter wear to go for a walk? How can my mother lose her pocketbook in our backyard and have no clue where it is? (Thanks to God, I found it at the back of our yard the next week. How can she write checks to her church and in one month give them almost all of her Social Security check and not remember doing that? How can my mother scream at me—her daughter—who is trying to take care of her and has been taking care of her through the years and not even understand or realize that she is screaming? How can? How can? How can? How can? And, thus continues our lives hourly.

Countryside Manor, July 1995

It is two weeks that I would rather choose to forget. But without this time, the ten months to follow would have been harder to accept.

July 19, 1995

I spend the day preparing Mother's clothes and personal belongings to be moved to Countryside Manor. We talk throughout the day about her moving there. I know that she does not comprehend that this is going to be permanent. The deal I have with John is that he come and get Mother late in the afternoon and let her spend the night with his family. Emotionally I cannot move her from our house to

Countryside Manor. I cannot let her go from here. He has agreed to do this for me. I have a neighbor come over and stay with Mother while I go and pick up some last-minute items that I have forgotten. When I return, they are sitting in our backyard in the Adirondack chairs under the old oak tree. I get out of my car and just stand and look at my mother. Against the backdrop of the beautiful flowers she loves so much, all appears to be at peace.

My heart breaks. I know that this is the last time I will see her sitting peacefully in our yard—the yard she loves and has cared for—the yard that has given her so much happiness—the yard outside her dream home. I cry out to God. "Why, God? Is there not another way? Why must Mother's life come to an end like this? I know in my heart that God has no answer for me. He is just as upset as I am that one of his beloved children must suffer.

My neighbor leaves, and Mother and I go inside. We cry together many times today. I finish organizing her things, but will not pack them until she is gone. I pack a small bag of essentials for Mother to take to John's house. As the time nears for her to go, I can hardly hold myself together. I feel guilty for not being able to keep her here and safe, and yet, I know there is no way I can continue to provide for her care. Alzheimer's Disease is bigger than any of us want to admit. It storms, it consumes, and it destroys, anything in its path. It takes a loving family relationship and creates strangers.

John arrives. He takes Mother's bag to the car. I hold Mother tight and tell her that I love her and that I will see her early in the morning. John helps her to the car. I come back inside and stand at the dining room window to watch them leave. As the car backs out of the driveway, I cry hysterically knowing that Mother will never be here in our home again. A part of my world comes crashing down as never before. "My God, why does this have to happen to us?" Again, there are no answers and at this point, no acceptance. I finish packing Mother's things. I cry so much that I actually feel sick. I almost call and tell John to bring her back home. But, I know that I cannot do this. I know that I have to go through with this. I am emotionally and physically drained.

July 20, 1995

I awaken at 4:30 a.m. I get up and fix a pot of coffee. Four cups later I shower, dress and head for John's house. Upon arriving, I find Carolyn and John extremely upset over Mother's behavior. Mother has been up during the night thinking she is at the beach. She and John had an argument and Carolyn had to get up and try to calm them both. I find Mother in the bathroom trying to bathe and dress herself. During the night she wet the bed. I help her change, bathe, and dress. I fix her a bowl of cereal and get her medication. I guess John and Carolyn have not understood what I have been living through on a daily basis. At 8 a.m. we leave for Countryside Manor.

Mother is in good humor as we ride her to her new home. I maintain my composure as I talk of the friends she will meet there and of the visits and trips we can still take together. We arrive and take Mother in. We sit in the Living Room until the Director comes. We then take Mother back to her room—unpack her things. I take her back to the living room while John takes the bags to the car. I do not want her to see us take them out. We chat with other residents, and finally, the Director comes to get me to sign papers and write a check. I hug Mother. I tell her how much I love her. She hugs me and says, "It's okay Honey. I am going to be okay, and so are you. I love you dearly." I leave her talking with other ladies who live there. After the rest of the papers are signed, and the business end is taken care of, I leave without trying to see Mother again. I cry all the way home.

On my way home, I make one stop. I stop at the grocery store and buy a quart of milk and a six-pack of beer. I want beer in my refrigerator for the first time in my life. I guess I just need to say to myself that I am going to do as I please from here on out. I still have so much anger directed toward all that has happened to Mother that this is my way of getting even. I have tried so hard to contain my anger through this whole ordeal, and now I must "get on" with my life. In my heart, I know that I am not trying to get rid of Mother, but rather to rid myself of the horrible disease that has consumed both of our lives.

The next two weeks were weeks of physical freedom. I wake up, sit in the den drinking my coffee thinking, "This is great. Finally, I will not be disturbed with some crazy talk. I have nothing to explain to anyone. I can just drink my coffee and read the paper in peace."

Of course, the other part of me already misses my mother. I want her back as she was before the storm. I want her to come home a whole being—just as much as she wants to come home. The phone calls from her are unbelievable. Mother calls and curses me for taking her to Countryside Manor. She accuses me of dumping her there. She accuses me of never loving her for if I loved her, I would come and get her. She says that she would not leave someone she loves in a place like this.

The second night Mother is at Countryside Manor, she escapes over the back fence and takes a hike up the highway. Fortunately, they are able to locate her and return her safely. She becomes physically and verbally abusive to the staff. I cringe when I come in and head for the answering machine.

If Mother does not get me on the telephone, she calls John's house in a tirade. The call Mother made to me this afternoon is the worst. After cursing and screaming she says, " I will loathe and despise you until the day that I die." These words tear my heart wide open. I cannot go and see her for ten days. The Director says that this is best. So here I am unable to even try to make things better for her.

The second weekend at Countryside Manor, Mother calls the police. The police come to Countryside Manor. Mother accuses the staff of beating her, pushing her down a flight of stairs, stealing her pocketbook and her car.

Fortunately, there are no stairs at Countryside Manor, and Mother never had a car there. She does look like she has been through a war zone. The staff has had to restrain her to keep her from being physically abusive and keep her from climbing the fence to escape. I can hardly believe the stories.

Three weeks ago I had to practically hold her up to walk her around the block. The staff at Countryside Manor call me and call Mother's doctor. She is so aggressive that they need to put her on medication. This they do.

Later in the day, the nurse calls me to let me know they have restrained Mother in a Gerry chair for her safety. The vision in my mind is horrifying. I ask myself, "What have you done to your Mother?" They still will not let me come and see her. During the next two days, the staff adjusts her medication until she is able to walk again.

A day later, just two weeks and one day from her arrival at Countryside Manor, Mother falls and breaks her hip. The story that they tell is that Mother had gone to bed. She got up to go to the bathroom. Going back to her room, she became confused and went into the wrong room. She fell to the floor. I have been out to dinner. I returned home at 10 p.m. There is a message on the answering machine from the Director of Countryside Manor. I call her back immediately.

She has called an ambulance, and they are going to transport Mother to Anderson Medical Center. I called my close and wonderful friend, Suzanne. I have had too much to drink and need a ride to the hospital. I called John's house. No one is at home. I leave a message for them to come as soon as they can. Suzanne arrives, and we leave for the hospital.

The whole time, Suzanne and I wait for the ambulance to arrive my mind races. Remembering the last conversation I had with Mother, I do not know what kind of reception to expect from her. The ambulance pulls up, and they unload the stretcher. When I walk over to her and take her hand, her sweet smile comes over her face and even through the pain she says, "I love you, Honey. They told me you would be here." I say, "I love you too, Mother." With these words, my world becomes okay again. For just a moment, Mother is back with me. Thus ends Mother's brief journey at Countryside Manor.

Anderson Medical Center
August 4, 1995 to September 5, 1995

We go into the Emergency Room with Mother and the emergency crew. She is in excruciating pain, crying, agitated, and not being fully able to understand what is happening to her. John arrives in about an hour. I let him walk Suzanne to her car so that she can go home. By now, it is almost midnight.

Many doctors come in and out of the room. They

take Mother to x-ray and verify their suspicion that her hip is indeed broken. An orthopedic doctor, Dr. Holmes, comes and talks with us. Surgery is a must for Mother. If she has the surgery the next day, he feels they can have her up within a week and walking again. Without the surgery, she will be confined to a bed and will die within a short period of time. Mother will be in pain the rest of her life. With these options presented, we consent for her to have the surgery. It will be scheduled for the following morning.

The biggest fear I have for Mother is her low platelets. It takes weeks for a small cut to heal. I do not see how they can cut her, repair her hip, and not let her bleed to death. Or how can they keep her from developing an infection after the surgery with the period of time it will take for her to heal? How do they think they can have her up and walking in a week when she is so disoriented, confused, and agitated? All of these questions are a part of my thinking. But I am not a doctor. And I have been told that Mother will suffer the rest of her life without surgery. I must put my questions aside and trust the doctors who are making the medical calls.

At 1 a.m., John takes me home so that I can shower and bring my car back to the hospital. I know we are in for the long haul with Mother. She cannot be left alone. She is extremely agitated and in so much pain. I arrive back at the hospital at 2:30 a.m. and let John go home. Mother tries continually to get out of bed. She hits and claws at me. She yells at me, and there is no reasoning with her. She cannot comprehend that she has a broken hip and cannot walk. We make it through the night.

The next morning at 7:30 a.m., John comes back. Suzanne and Peggy (Mother's niece and my cousin) come. Mother is scheduled for surgery at 11 a.m.

As the time for the surgery draws closer, I cannot stop holding Mother and letting her know how much I love her. I am sure that the guilt of placing her in a rest home has caught up with me. No matter how I try to intellectualize the situation, there is always some guilt. By placing Mother there, I somehow feel responsible for her broken hip. I can only resolve my guilt by holding her and loving her for what possibly could be the last time. Her platelet problem is foremost in my mind. I also admit thinking that it would be a blessing if she did not make it through the surgery. Maybe that is selfish, but it is a thought that would bring her a peaceful exit from the demented state she is forced to live in. So many things race through my mind.

John and I go with her to the holding area of the operating room. I continue to hold her and say my goodbyes as best I can. I should invest in Kleenex stock! The anesthesiologist comes out and talks to us. He begins to take Mother's vitals. When he listens to her heart, he becomes concerned. He asks if she has ever had a heart murmur. We say that we have never been aware of one. He has some concerns about the possibility of a leaky heart valve but assures us that they will monitor her very closely. We both say our final goodbyes and leave to go to the surgery waiting room. It should take no more than three hours.

Surgical waiting rooms are no fun. I feel estranged from John and have difficulty trying to communicate with him. I am exhausted. Several times, Suzanne tries to rescue me and take me to the smoking area, but I am unable to get away. Oh, how I wish I could just go off by myself and cry myself into oblivion. The emotional effects of the past months are catching up with me.

The minutes pass very slowly. After three hours, I go to the desk and inquire if they have heard anything regarding Mother. After about three-and-a-half hours, they ask us to go down to the operating room and talk to the anesthesiologist. All the way to the OR, I keep thinking that Mother must have died. Why else would they send us back there?

When we arrive, the anesthesiologist is nowhere

to be found. We go back to the surgical waiting room, and they page him. In another forty-five minutes, we are led to Cardiac Intensive Care where we discover that Mother never had surgery. She has been in Cardiac Intensive Care experiencing cardiac arrhythmia. They call a cardiac specialist who later arrives and runs tests. Mother is hooked up to all kinds of machines and looks like death warmed over. She is doped up and really cannot respond at this point. I go back to the surgical waiting room to let Suzanne and Peggy know what has happened, and that they should go home. John and I decide that for now, Mother is in good hands.

I rest at home until 6:30 p.m. I return to find Mother in the same condition. They have scheduled a heart echo test for Sunday. Until then, they keep her hooked up to machines and carefully monitor her condition. I stay with her for a little while but know that there is nothing I can do. I leave to go home.

The heart echo test reveals that she has three leaky heart valves. Mother's doctor explains that the fibrillations heard in her heart were from this. He explains that when the fibrillations begin, it takes them a long time to stop. This can send someone into cardiac arrest. Mother needs to remain in Cardiac Intensive Care until she is stable. I feel safe with her there and once again go home.

It is Monday. John goes to Countryside Manor to get Mother's things and bring them to me. I take a few minutes today to unpack them while taking an hour off from hospital duty.

When I find Mother's devotional book, I find the first card I sent her at Countryside Manor. It reads:

Hi, Mom

Today is Friday, and you are on my mind and in my heart. I hope your new home and your new friends are helping to take good care of you. God blessed our lives so much by helping to find such a nice place for you to live. The race set before us—with all its adjustments, it will not be easy. My prayer to God is that you will continue to run the race set before you with all the grace and beauty of the years before. I love you and want you to feel this love today. Call me if you just want to talk. I plan to come and see you on Sunday, July 30th.

Love, Nancy

P.S. Smile!

I cry when I find the note. Of all the phone calls and all of the lashing out at me, of all the hatred expressed, the bottom line is that Mother kept my note. She not only kept it, but she kept it in her devotional book. That meant something to her, or it would not have been in her special book.

At some moment in time, I have to think that her mind had perceived the love that I had sent and that is all that matters. Maybe she was given just a moment to perceive that love. For often in the midst of a storm there is a moment of peace—perhaps a moment was all Mother was able to comprehend, and I am grateful to have hopefully given her that moment.

Mother has stabilized and is moved to a heart monitored private room. She is pretty much out of it. She just lies in bed and either hums or sings hymns. It is comforting to listen to her. John and I stay with her together until early afternoon. John has to leave, and I stay on.

Mother's doctor comes in. He says that while she is stable now, there are no guarantees that she will remain so. If her heart starts fibrillating and will not stop, she will go into cardiac arrest. With a patient in Mother's condition, that could be within the next minute, or it could take years. It is not a predictable situation. The mortality rate for Mother with surgery would be 50 percent. The mortality rate for her without surgery would be 50 percent.

Dr. Holmes, the orthopedic doctor, comes by later in the day. John and I talked over the weekend and decided not to put Mother through surgery. In the mental condition she is in and now the physical condition, we do not believe she could survive surgery. If she did, indeed, survive, in all probability, she would not walk again—despite what the orthopedic doctor says.

I convey our thoughts to Dr. Holmes. He is quite hostile. "Why would you want your mother not to walk again? Do you know that this is writing her death sentence?" Doctors can be so cruel. I keep explaining about Mother's platelets and her heart condition. I keep explaining about her Alzheimer's Disease. I keep explaining the percentages of mortality rates given to us by her doctor. Dr. Holmes tells me that I only have three days to change my mind. "If you love your mother you will. After three days, you can write her off. You are killing her anyway." By this time, I have an extreme dislike for this man. He does order Mother's leg to be put in traction.

In a week, they release Mother from the heart monitor room and move her to the orthopedic floor. I have not seen or heard from the orthopedic doctor, Dr. Holmes, since our conversation last week.

When they move Mother, they remove the traction. Two days later, I question a nurse as to why Mother's leg is not still in traction. She says that she does not know—as a nurse, she feels like the traction should be continued.

I ask for Dr. Holmes to be paged and sent to Mother's room. When he enters the room, I ask him why Mother's leg in no longer in traction. He turns and looks at her and says, "Your daughter has decided for you not to have surgery. Because of that decision, you will never walk again so traction would do you no good. You will live out your life in a bed, and a wheelchair and will have to go to a nursing home. As a result of this, you will develop pneumonia and die. I guess this is what your daughter wants for you by making this decision."

I look at Dr. Holmes and say, "Excuse me. I am over here. Do not ever say those things to my mother or me in that manner again. You never even came back to see her. You gave us three days. It has been a week. Furthermore, get out of this room and do not ever come back!"

I am livid. Mother, in her confused state, does not seem to understand what Dr. Holmes said. I hope she didn't. The bottom line is that he never should have said those things to me in front of her, much less to her. The callousness of mankind continues to astound me.

Two days later, Dr. Holmes has Mother moved off his floor. Mother is moved to the cancer floor which is the floor most used by Mother's primary care doctor.

With her in a private room, I am forced to hire twenty-four-hour private duty nursing assistants to stay with her. Mother cannot be in the room by herself. Cognitively, she has no clue how to ring the call bell for help. I cannot take a chance on her trying to get out of bed.

Most times, Mother cannot comprehend that she has a broken hip and is not able to get up. I am fortunate to have excellent CNAs with her. They really care for her during this period of time.

I defy you to find a nurse on the floor who can tell you anything about your mother when you arrive in the afternoon. I especially defy you to make contact with a doctor. So, day-to-day, you flounder, wondering what is being done for your mother and wondering where to go from here.

One afternoon a nurse stopped me as I came off the elevator. She wanted to talk with me. We go around the corner from the nurses' station. She asks me why I opted not to have hip surgery for Mother. I explain the total situation to her. She put her arms around me and says, "If it makes you feel any better, you made the right decision.

*Please do not tell anyone that I said that to you.
I just wanted you to know." Oh, how good that
makes me feel!*

*Mother has been on pain medication, and her
pain seems to be lessening as the days grow longer.
Her doctor put her back in traction after being out
of it for three weeks. I have gone back to work.*

*I leave work in the afternoon, go to the hospital,
usually get dinner from the snack shop, and have
dinner with Mother. Or I go after work, spend time
up until dinner time, go home, and go back in the
evening to take her some ice cream or cheesecake.*

*These are long days, and I am not sure where
to go from here. Occasionally, I have contact with
John, but those contacts are few and far between. I
do not know if he goes and spends time with Mother.
He does not share this with me. The impact of my
being alone and making life and death decisions
about her is frightening. And, alone, I am. For all
practical purposes, I have lost my family and my
church at this time. I still have friends who call and
who care. This is a comfort. There just is nothing
they can do at this point.*

*My mind is consumed with the lack of support
from our church. When Mother was still able to go
to church, members would come to me and ask about
her. They knew something was wrong. They could tell*

in her conversations and in her actions. I confirmed their suspicions when I had the opportunity to talk with them away from Mother.

Many members talked with me. Only a few ever called or came to see Mother. She must have been lonelier than I am. Just the other day, I chastised our deacon to our Minister, Allen. "He has not so much as made a telephone call to our house since Mother went to the hospital." Allen said that he was going to talk with him—I asked him not to do that, feeling that if a deacon needed a reminder from the minister to contact one of his families and visit them, then the visit was not genuine.

The next week, Mother's deacon came to the hospital one afternoon. It was all I could do to be civilized to him. It really makes me angry. I truly expected members of our church to be supportive. Mother and our family have been active members of our church for forty-five years. I can count on my fingers the number of people in the church who have come to see her in the hospital. And, not even one person has called our house to see if I am dead or alive. I guess when you stop going to church, you are written off as dead.

For all practical purposes, I feel dead. My soul really cannot find much reason for continuing to live, except that I know my mother needs me. I cannot give up, no matter how rough the road gets. But, believe me, I do have thoughts of giving up, rolling over, and dying.

I arrive at the hospital this afternoon to find Mother tied to the bed with wrist cuffs. I am devastated. The CNA staying with her said they had to restrain her. She was insistent on getting out of bed and tried to hurt the nurses when they would not let her get up. I have seen Mother verbally abusive. I have seen her try to hit me. But I have not actually seen her hurt someone. How can you possibly believe that your mother would try to claw someone's eyes, or to hit them, or hurt them? But as the days wear on, I do see this behavior myself. I even learn how to tie the cuffs, and there are many times that it is better to tie them than to see her struggle so.

This is one of the hardest things I have had to do. Just imagine tying your Mother to a bed and leaving her. How do I cope? I do not know. Maybe I don't cope. Maybe I just get through it one day at a time.

One couple in our church lives in my neighborhood. They are so supportive of me. Their names are Gary and Martha Bass, and they are two of the most loving people I have ever met.

Martha goes to see Mother and takes her chocolate ice cream. They have me to dinner to make sure that I eat. One Saturday afternoon, I stop by their house. Martha asks me if I think Mother would like a teddy bear to hold and love while she spends so much of her time in bed? I tell her that I do not know, but it is worth a try.

Martha gives me a bear that she bought for her mother when she was in a nursing home. I take the bear home and write TJ on its ribbon. TJ is the name of Mother's cat, and the bear is similar in color to TJ. I take the bear to Mother. She is elated.

At this time, Mother has a bar over her bed so that she can pull herself up. It does not take her long to figure out a way to place TJ in that bar and swing him. She derives so much pleasure from this activity. She often sleeps with TJ and becomes upset if he has fallen and she cannot find him. "Thanks, Martha, for giving TJ back to Mother!"

The fourth week in the hospital, I receive a call at school one afternoon. It is the call I dreaded. The social worker at the hospital has found an available nursing home bed. She wants me to visit there today and let her know this afternoon what I think.

It on the other side of town—not in a very desirable neighborhood. But, I go. When I walk in, the smell of urine is so strong I nearly vomit. The Director of Admissions comes and takes me on a tour. I cannot believe what my eyes are seeing.

Back in her office, she explains fees and such to me. I discuss Mother with her. I tell he how supportive I plan to be—visiting daily. She tells me that they prefer that their families do not visit daily. At that point, I have had enough. I leave telling her that I will talk with the social worker at the hospital and will have her call tomorrow.

We have to either accept or reject the placement by the end of today. I cry all the way to the hospital. What if we do not take it and the hospital releases Mother to a nursing home outside Charlotte? What would I do? Can I continue looking and find something on my own?

By the time I reach the parking deck of the hospital, I know that I will not let Mother go there. I would not even let my cats be placed there. My God, man's inhumanity to man! This is on Wednesday. I find the social worker and tell her of my experience there and absolutely refuse for Mother to be placed there.

While talking with her, I can still smell the stench of urine on my clothes. I tell the social worker that I intend to spend the next two days finding Mother a nursing home to go to. I visit with Mother for a while, go home, and begin my research.

Morning finds me beginning in the outskirts of our city with visitations to Nursing Homes. Throughout the day, I wind my way into the inner city. My last stop is at Meadow Brook, an older Nursing Home in a beautiful part of our city. I talked with the Administrator and the Director there. They review Mother's records, tell me they have a room, and will accept her as a resident! They tell me she can come tomorrow! I fill out all the necessary papers and leave to let the hospital know I have found a Nursing Home placement for Mother! I went home and called John to let him know of my success. I ask him to meet me at Meadow Brook the next morning as the hospital would be transporting Mother to her new home.

September 5 to September 9, 1995

On Tuesday, September 5, 1995, I awaken to the sounds of music on my radio. The clock tells me that it is 5 a.m. The song is one that I will never forget. It is a song sung by Colin Raye.

If it all falls apart,

I will know deep in my heart,

the only dream that mattered had come true.

In this life, I was loved by you.

This song had such deep significance in my life when I lost Howard, and my friends moved to Texas.

And now, it would ever remind me of the significance of this day. Life has fallen apart. All the good seems lost. My soul cries out for peace—peace for myself and peace for my mother.

Nothing about the world I live in seems to hold good anymore. But the bottom line in all of this should be remembered as in the words of this song—"in this life, I was loved by you." And not only was, but I am still loved by you, Mother. Most importantly I go on loving you and somehow will find a way to make your life as easy as possible until the end. God gave me to you. You gave your love to me unconditionally. Your love gave me life. And now I will strive each and every day to fulfill our mission—whatever that may be."

I say a prayer of thanksgiving to God this morning for the beauty of the world He has given us to live in. I say a prayer of thanksgiving to God for the beautiful Mother He gave to me and for all that we have shared through the years. Not everyone is given this privilege. I ask for strength to go through this day and through the days, weeks, months, and perhaps years ahead. I ask for guidance, not knowing how very much I will need that guidance through the turbulence of nursing home life. Most of all, I ask for peace. And I arise with the dawn to begin a new phase in our lives.

There is an excitement about this day. As horrible as it is in reality, I have to feel that it is good. I feel that I have found a good nursing home for my mother. I know that I have found one close to home and work so I can still be a part of my mother's daily life.

Many of my friends who know that I am placing her in a nursing home today have replied, "Good, now you can get on with your life." Obviously, they have not been through this ordeal. Mother is still very much a part of my life. She always will be. Just because she is going to live in a nursing home does not mean that my responsibility ends. No, contrary. It only begins at a new depth. I know this, even on this first day. I pledge to continue to care for her and see that her life somehow continues to experience dignity. That pledge will demand countless hours of my time. I know this, but love knows no bounds. That love was placed in my heart on March 22, 1948, when I became Mother's daughter. Never in my life has it ever been taken away for any reason. And never in my life will I take it away from my mother.

And so on this day, I place my mother in Meadow Brook Nursing Home. I go to Meadow Brook a couple of hours prior to her arriving by ambulance from the hospital to talk to the Admissions Director, Faye. We go over Legal Representations, Terminations of

Agreements, Enforcement of Agreements, Private Pay, Medicare, Medicaid, Bed Holds, Personal Funds, Consent for Treatments, Residents Records, Residents Duties, Transfers/Discharges, Resident Rights, and Advance Directives. I am alone in all of this.

I asked John to meet me here, but he is late. I sign many more papers to include a statement of my Registered Power of Attorney, accepting Dr. Lawrence as Mother's physician (as her current physician refused to continue seeing her), Admission Agreement, and Authorization to Obtain Medical information. It is almost too much for the mind to comprehend. But, as Power of Attorney, it is up to me to see that everything is taken care of.

I have taken a copy of Mother's Living Will and for the first time have to say to someone what her wishes are. I never realized just how important that paper was until now. Waiting in Faye's office while she processes some of the papers, John comes. A family in his church had surgery, and he is sorry that he is late

John asks, "Where is Mother? Why is she not here yet?" How does he think that I would know? He cannot stay long and must get back to the hospital. At that moment from Faye's door, I see Mother being wheeled in on a stretcher. We greet her and

John leaves. She is in a good mood but confused about where she is.

I have kept the private duty CNAs for three days to help Mother adjust to her new place of residence. Mother is used to them. We go up in the elevator to the third floor where her room will be. They are in the process of moving another resident out. Confusion is at a max.

We transferred Mother to the bed nearest the hallway until the move could be completed. The CNA arrives shortly. Her name is Martha. She is perhaps the most compassionate person I have ever known. She has been with Mother through much of her hospital stay—even requesting double shifts many days to stay with her.

We have created a bond of love between us through the care of Mother. God is good to give us people like Martha. We now have all of Mother's belongings in bags all over the room. Chaos reigns. The day goes on, and nothing gets any better.

Finally at 5:30 in the afternoon, Martha begs me to go home. She is planning to stay all night with Mother. I am ready to drop. Martha promises me that she will complete the move for Mother and arrange all of her belongings for me. I hug her and leave Mother for her first night in Meadow Brook. I am grateful for Martha and feel good that she will be with Mother. I can rest easy tonight.

The first few days of life at Meadow Brook are a rude awakening. Mother is bed-bound, and thus all of my experiences happen within a confined space. The larger nursing home picture will come to me later, I am sure.

At this point in Mother's life, she has become incontinent. She still has a catheter in place. She has a pad on her sheet/mattress but continues to have BMs in bed. I ask a nursing assistant if I should get her some Depends, or how do they handle incontinence? She explains that the facility furnishes diapers for the residents. I ask for one to be put on Mother. Do you know what it is like to ask for diapers for your mother? No one can describe the feeling you have inside when you realize that until the day your Mother dies, she will now wear diapers.

This is on Wednesday. On Thursday, Friday, and Saturday, I continue to ask for diapers to be kept on Mother. Her gowns are being brought home caked with BM. Her footies are caked with BM. I feel sick with every load of laundry I bring home.

Mother also has BM on her hands, legs, and feet during these days. I don't think I have ever been more devastated. The nursing assistant who comes in to clean Mother has no idea that she has a broken hip and needs to be turned with the bed pads—not by pushing on her hips and listening to her scream out in pain.

I inform the nursing assistants that Mother needs her food cut up in tiny pieces as she is having difficulty chewing and swallowing, and she needs assistance with feeding. She is not able to feed herself.

Mother is very agitated on Saturday and in so much pain. I leave her at 1 p.m. to come home and do her laundry. I return at 3 p.m. to be with her for a little while. From 3 until 5 p.m. no one even comes in to check on her.

I ring at 5 p.m. to let them know that Mother needs to be changed. She has had a BM. I ask again for a diaper to be kept on her. Supper comes around 7:05 p.m. No one comes to help her eat. I can only get her to eat six spoonfuls of food. She does drink a half a glass of tea. She cannot stay awake. She cannot chew and swallow to eat. I check her diaper that I am finally able to get for her. She is still dry, but her vaginal area is caked with BM from the five o'clock cleaning.

Welcome to nursing home life. I am exhausted and go home. I am livid at the lack of care thus far at this "good" nursing home. I spend the next few hours at my computer writing my complaints about Mother's care and plan to deliver it to the Director of Nursing on Monday morning. This is just not acceptable care. And, to date, I have not seen one staff member other than a nursing assistant even come near my mother.

I know that I am new at all of this, but with Mother's medical problems, I just feel I need some answers as to the care they plan to provide for her. Thus my venture begins. The rest of my story I will tell month by month. There are parts of this story that still amaze me even now. Man's inhumanity to man truly exists—even amidst love and concern. I guess the most important thing to remember as you follow along through our journey is that in all of the following excerpts, Mother was in a "good" nursing home. God be with all residents and families for whom this is not possible.

September 10 to September 27, 1995
Sunday, September 10, 1995

I arrive at Meadow Brook at 11 a.m. Mother had a bath, but she has BM in her diaper. I ask for washcloths/ towels and a fresh diaper. This is the first time I clean and change my mother's diaper. I cry the whole time. I also take her dentures out and brush and clean them as there is food caked on them from breakfast.

Her lunch comes at 12:15 and is placed on her bedside tray. No one comes and offers to help feed her. I feed her.

At 12:45, I ring the call bell to get a bedpan for her. At 1:05, no one has come. I find her a bedpan and put her on it myself.

At 1:10, I ring the call bell to get assistance getting her off the bedpan and to help get her clean. At 1:35, help comes. The entire time I am with Mother, no one even checks in on her except to give her medication.

I leave around 2 p.m.

I come back at 4:15 p.m. Mother is in bed, her diaper undone, her gown partially off, her sheet has come off the mattress and is matted under her. There is BM everywhere. I go and ask for washcloths, towels, a fresh diaper, and a fresh sheet. I clean Mother completely, put on a fresh gown, and sit with her as she sleeps until dinner.

Dinner arrives at 6:45 p.m. No one offers to help her eat. I try. Mother only eats a few bites of food and drinks a little tea. I let the nurse know that it is past time for her medication. She brings it to me, and I give it to Mother.

From 4:15 p.m. until 7:15 p.m., no one checks on her. The CNA whom I have come to love dearly,

Jean, does put a sign above Mother's bed that the family requests a diaper be kept on Mother. It is very disheartening to see Mother neglected as she has been today, but I must go back to work on Monday. I guess I will just have to hope that things will be better for her tomorrow.

Monday, September 11, 1995

I arrive at Meadow Brook at 4 p.m. Mother has her call bell on playing with the cord. She says she needs a bedpan. I leave the call bell on because her diaper, which is only lying underneath her like a pad, is caked with BM.

At 4:30, the nurse comes, and I explain that Mother needed a bedpan, but that it is now too late. I need help cleaning her. Two CNAs come. Mother's bed is soaked. We change everything and bathe her. I request again that a diaper not only be placed on Mother but that it be snapped in place.

Checking Mother after they leave, I discover that her vaginal area is still caked with BM. I go and ask for a washcloth and clean her myself. Mother is extremely confused by this time.

Her dentures are caked with food from two previous meals. I take them out, clean them, and put them back in. I sit with her, and she calms down and goes to sleep.

I leave to go home at 5 p.m. I return at 6:10 p.m. Mother is awake and sweet. Her dinner comes at 6:50 p.m. I feed her and have to ask for a bib. I leave at 7:40 p.m. to go home to rest. Diapers, cleanliness, teeth brushed, etc. The simple things in life are sometimes the hardest

BM under Mother's fingernails is not tolerable under any circumstances. I just cannot understand. What happened to the resident's first right—the right to dignity? On this day, also, I did deliver my first 'letter of concern' to the Nursing Director at Meadow Brook. The concerns expressed were those regarding diapers being kept on Mother, proper cleaning for BM and incontinent episodes, dentures cleaned after all meals to prevent food from dislodging from them and choking her in her sleep (she is a mouth breather), assistance with meals, and fingernails cleaned as a part of regular bathing routine each day. The Director of Nursing was very understanding, and within an hour of talking with her, a meeting was scheduled for the next day with the staff and me.

Tuesday, September 12, 1995

I arrive at Meadow Brook at 3:30 p.m. for my meeting. There must be fifteen people in the room.

I am used to these meeting because of conferences I am involved in at school. Otherwise, I would probably have turned and walked out of the room!

We discuss my areas of concern and each discipline speaks to the way they plan to handle these concerns. I leave the meeting feeling better and somehow knowing that Mother's care will improve.

I visit with Mother from 4:15 until 6:55 p.m. I feed her dinner. The CNA checks in on her once around 5 p.m. Mother had her medication at 6:15 and fell asleep. She was in a great mood today.

Wednesday, September 13, 1995

I arrive at Meadow Brook at 4 p.m. Mother is asleep. She never wakes up enough to talk except to say that she is cold. She had spilled either coffee or tea sometime earlier—probably lunch. It has soaked through her quilt, bedspread, sheet, and gown. It is still damp. She also has BM in her diaper. I ring for the CNA to strip her bed and change her

The CNA and I clean Mother and put clean linen and a clean spread on her bed. I leave at 5:45 p.m. to go to a PTA supper at school.

Thursday, September 14, 1995

I arrive at Meadow Brook at 3:15 p.m. Mother has had a BM. The CNA helps me change her. The CNA says that she did not know that Mother needs help with feeding, but that she would help her with her evening meal.

Friday, September 15, 1995

I arrive at Meadow Brook at 3:15 p.m. Mother is asleep. The CNA says that she will clean her as soon as her cart arrives. I am sick and go home to try and rest.

Saturday and Sunday, September 16 and 17, 1995

All is well. All is clean. I feed Mother lunch and supper on these days. She eats very little. She sleeps most of the time. I notice her right leg is not moving when I bend her leg at the knee, and the skin hangs at the back and looks very shriveled. Her leg is only the size of the bone with skin hanging. I must ask the physical therapist or doctor to look at this. Am I the only person noticing these things with Mother? I guess the truth about nursing homes is true—people only come here to die. What else is there to do?

Monday, September 25, 1995

I arrive at Meadow Brook at 3:30 p.m. Mother is soaked and has had a BM. She has used four gowns since 7 p.m. last night. Big chunks of chicken are still in her mouth from lunch. Chicken and green beans are all over her bed. The CNA helps me clean Mother. I leave a note regarding checking her mouth after meals for food. I come home at 4:10 p.m.

Wednesday, September 27, 1995

I arrive at Meadow Brook at 6:15 p.m. No one is helping Mother eat. Juice and tea are spilled all over her blanket, sheet, gown, and bed. Her food is not cut up. She has an extremely large portion of pancake in her mouth. She is going to sleep and trying to mouth breathe with this food in her mouth.

I ring for the nurse. The CNA comes ten minutes later. She is upset with another CNA who left Mother like this. We clean Mother, put on a fresh diaper, and put a new pad on her bed. I strip her bed and put clean linen on. I put a fresh gown on her and add another note at the head of her bed that she needs assistance with meals.

I plan to go to the Director of Nursing tomorrow with another "letter of concern." As a result of all of this, Mother had no dinner today. I did get her some ice cream and help her eat.

October 1995

It is now October. The Financial Administrator at Meadow Brook greets me in the hallway and asks to talk with me. It is time to begin the application process for Medicaid for Mother.

I am at a loss. I know that Mother's money—what little she had—is going rapidly. Nursing home care is expensive!! The private duty CNA expense was phenomenal and took more money than I ever imagined, not to mention the hospital bills. People are under the impression that Medicare and Supplemental Policies will pay for everything. Not! I found out the hard way that this is certainly not true. I tell the Financial Administrator that I will comply with her wishes and begin the Medicaid process.

I leave really not knowing where to turn. My mother's roommate's daughter is going through the same thing and advises me to contact the hospital rather than going through the main Social Services office. I do this the next day.

Mrs. Jones becomes my contact person. She sets up an interview with me for the following day. She gives me a list of all of the papers and financial records I need to bring. What an avalanche of paperwork.

I gather all the records in the evening and haul them to work the next day. After work, I take them to Mrs. Jones. We go over them one by one, accounting for every penny of Mother's money along the way for the past three years.

Mother and I had planned and transferred some of her money into my name, but too late. The 'look back' period is three years, and that was the beginning of our transfers.

I am honest with Mrs. Jones and show her every document. At this point, Mother has approximately $4000 in her possession. Mrs. Jones explains how the process for approval can take up to ninety days, so I should go ahead and apply for Medicaid. During that time, I can be 'spending down' Mother's money to $2000—the amount she may have at the time of acceptance.

The money must be spent on Mother. I ask Mrs. Jones what in the world I would spend $2000 on in ninety days for her. She suggests things like a TV for her room, a nice lounge chair, etc. I begin to explain that Meadow Brook provides a TV and that Mother has a broken hip and cannot sit in a chair. Mrs. Jones quickly quiets me. "Don't tell me things like that," she says. "Just spend the money, and we will say that your mother needed the items."

What an introduction to the Government Welfare waste system! No wonder it's going broke! It would seem to me that the money would be better used to set up an account for Mother to help buy robes, gowns, and toiletries; things Mother will need along the way, rather than going for the 'big spend' items which she does not need—and I certainly don't! Oh, well, I have at least ninety days to figure all of this out.

Two weeks later I receive a phone call from Mrs. Jones at work. Mother's application for Medicaid has been approved, and she must only have $2000 in her possession by noon tomorrow. I still show $4000 in Mother's account. Mrs. Jones suggests going out after work and getting rid of the money. Otherwise, the process will begin all over again.

I leave work feeling sick. I come home and begin thinking. What in the world will I spend $2000 on tonight that could help us? There just is nothing. It is so absurd.

At 7 p.m. I finally go to Circuit City and purchase a TV/VCR combo and an expensive camcorder. This comes to a little over $1200. I have yet more to get rid of. I buy another TV and have the store 'lump the cost' of the two TV's into one for government records.

I come home, have my neighbor help me unload my purchases into the house, collapse, and cry. Here I am by myself in a house with four TVs, two VCRs, and a camcorder I do not care anything about. I go to Mother's checkbook to record the purchases and

*subtract the money only to find that at some point I
have made a $1000 error and still need to get rid of
$1000 by tomorrow.*

*I write a check to John for $1000, listing it for
Christmas and birthday presents for his family for
the next year. Finally, at midnight, I collapse into
bed and cry myself to sleep. The weight of all of the
responsibility placed on me is too great. Slowly but
surely, the storm is creating rock slides in my life
from which I cannot escape.*

*The next afternoon, I go to Mrs. Jones' office. I
take all of my documentation with me. Mrs. Jones
has somehow lost all of the records I previously took
to her. I leave, go home, get my copies, and go back
to her office. I help her organize them once again
and let her make copies for herself. Mrs. Jones wants
to keep the originals, but I am far smarter than that!*

*Finally, at 6:45 p.m., the records are straight, and
Mother is finally approved for the great Government
Welfare waster program—Medicaid.*

*I feel relieved, not knowing that this great
program is not all it is cracked up to be. There
are hidden costs involved with nursing home care
that even this program does not cover. These I will
find out about along the way and learn lesson after
lesson about the financial responsibility for caring
for your parent in a nursing home setting.*

October 1 to October 6, 1995
Sunday, October 1, 1995

I arrive at Meadow Brook at 12:15 p.m. Mother had a BM. I go downstairs until lunch arrives at 12:45 p.m. Lunch is fried chicken. Mother cannot chew or swallow this. The CNA brings her extra soft food after I ask for the third time since Thursday if she can be put on a soft food diet

I am able to get her to eat two bites of cream potatoes and drink four sips of tea. She cannot manage a straw. She still has eggs in her mouth from breakfast. There is no bib or towel. I use paper towels as a bib. Mother's dentures are caked with food from breakfast. Her mouth is bleeding. Still, no one checks on her.

At 1:20 p.m., a CNA comes for her food tray. I tell her that Mother's mouth is bleeding. She says she will get the nurse.

At 1:30 p.m., Mother is still soaked and has BM. No one checks on her. No nurse at 2:20 p.m.

I ring again. The CNA comes and helps me clean Mother. I ask again for the nurse to check Mother's mouth. She is also complaining of extreme pain in her right shoulder. There is a bruise on her right arm, and there are fingerprints. Are people turning her using the pad? Can Mother's right shoulder be checked? I will ask the nurse these questions if she ever comes to check on the bleeding issue.

Forty-five minutes later, the nurse comes. At this time they inform me of an appointment at the orthopedic clinic on October 12th. I ask them to change it to the next week so that I can go with Mother.

I check her eating chart. It appears that she is eating 50 percent of her breakfast and most times 25 percent of her lunch and supper. I doubt the accuracy of this as four spoonfuls of food do not relate to 25 percent of a meal. I ask again for a soft diet.

I am informed that Mother is getting speech therapy for her memory. I know she has been evaluated but am not aware that she is receiving therapy—and expensive therapy at that. Memory is not an issue—chewing and swallowing is. I will check into this.

The nurse checks Mother's mouth and determines that her mouth may be bleeding due to irritated gums. The nurse says she will put a reminder note in Mother's chart to turn her with pads—not her arms and to clean her dentures after every meal. I go home to get some rest.

I come back at 5:05 p.m. Mother has been changed. Dirty diaper and pads are lying on the chair beside her bed. Her supper is a regular diet— and a hot dog at that! Why would anybody give her the worst food that can cause choking?

At 6:05 p.m., I go downstairs.

At 6:36 p.m., I come back to Mother's room. No one is there to help her eat. At 6:40 p.m., I feed her small bites of the hot dog with beans and a cup of fruit with whipped cream. She does drink almost all of her milk.

At 6:55 p.m., no one has even checked to see if she has eaten. The CNA begins picking up trays at 7 p.m. She has no comment on anyone helping Mother eat. I call for assistance at 7:05 p.m., as Mother needs to be changed. If I had not been here, how would Mother have eaten? If she had eaten, would she have choked to death on her hot dog? Would Mother have been changed? And this is a good nursing home.

Monday, October 2, 1995

I arrive at 4:15 p.m. I first drop my papers of concern off with Nursing Director before going upstairs. As I enter Mother's room, the smell of urine knocks me out. Mother's sheets, pad, diaper, and gown are wet and have been for some time. She has BM. I ring for help and in the meantime get a washcloth, towel, diaper, pad, sheet, and begin to clean Mother.

In this short period of time, I have learned that

if your loved one needs something in a nursing home, you might as well do it yourself. Mother's teeth have not been brushed today. I brought a new container, brush, and toothpaste yesterday. They have not been touched.

I talk to the nurses to let them know how I have found Mother. It is so sad that this has to happen. It really makes me wonder what happens when I am not here. Maybe I worry too much, but I must make sure that her needs are met at all times. BM dried on hands and under her fingernails is not acceptable at any time!

During this time, the Nursing Director and various Heads of Departments descend on Mother's room. They have read my paper of concern and want to meet with me on Wednesday, October 4th. I note on this day that Mother only weighs 107 pounds.

Wednesday, October 4, 1995

I meet with all people responsible for Mother's care. We discuss all facets of her care and address all of my concerns. I leave the meeting feeling like things will get better—or at least feeling that I have done all I can at this point.

Thursday, October 5, 1995

I arrive at Meadow Brook around 4 p.m. Mother is clean and changed. The nurse comes in to talk with me regarding bruises on Mother's arm. I note new bruises on her left hand and arm. Her dentures are caked with food. The nurse cleans these while I have Mother rinse to clear the food from her mouth.

The nurse practitioner has seen Mother and stopped her dosage of the drug Ativan. I talk with her by telephone. She wants to give it a couple of days to clear her system. I explain Mother's behavior when not on Ativan. If aggression or agitation present, I request that she be put back on Ativan.

I talk with all the nurses. They all agree. I inform all the nurses and the nurse practitioner that I am going out of town the next week and my friend, Joyce Deaton, will be filling in for me. I ask them to talk with her regarding any decisions that may have to be made for Mother. Joyce will know how to contact me if necessary. I am going to the beach for a week. I have to get away before I fall completely apart and am no good to anyone,

Joyce has graciously volunteered to help Mother and me. What an angel! She has her own plate full in caring for her own mother, but out of her love for her Aunt Mary Ann and for me, she comes to our rescue.

I am able to get Mother to drink a milkshake at 7:30 p.m. and to eat some ice cream. I have the nurse note both of these on her chart.

I leave at 8:30 p.m. I questioned the medication change while I will be away and it worries me somewhat that I will not be her to monitor changes in Mother. But, I get nowhere! I wish they would wait one week until I get back—but a brick wall!

Friday, October 6, 1995

I arrive at 3:45 p.m. Mother is asleep—very clean—very dry. She wakes up and asks me to sit with her on her bed. She is very loving and smiling, and she calls me Nancy!

We talk about our life together and how grateful to God she is for the blessing of that life we have shared. We talk about my upcoming beach trip. Mother seems happy for me to go and seems to remember Dave and Donna (my best friends from Texas).

I am an emotional basket case as it seems that Mother is saying her goodbyes to me once again. She cannot stop hugging and loving me. What a beautiful time of sharing with each other. These are the times I hold dear to my heart and feel thankful to God for moments of having her back with me. Just the fact that she knows me today as Nancy is a miracle!

The CNA checks on her two times while I am here. I leave at 4:30 p.m., as Mother wants to take a nap. As good as it is to be going away, I will miss her and worry about her until I come home. May God be with her and give her peace while I am away!

My trip to the beach is great! It is good to be with my friends in a normal environment having fun again. I talk with Joyce every day to check on Mother. It is just something I feel I must do. Things have been okay with her—there has not been a crisis that Joyce has not been able to handle, but all good things must end at one time or another. For me, it is now time to go back to the world of reality.

Back to reality means a trip to the orthopedic clinic as soon as I arrive back in town. Mother is transported by ambulance with me along to the Clinic. When we get to the floor where the doctor she was to see is located, Mother waits on the stretcher in the hall for thirty minutes.

The ambulance personnel keep saying that they must have their stretcher and have to go on another call. Finally, two nurses come and take Mother and me to the x-ray room. They ask me what Mother is being seen for. I explain that Meadow Brook wants an x-ray of her hip to determine if she is able to sit up at all or bear any weight on her leg.

The nurses proceed to plop Mother on the x-ray table so they can return the stretcher to the Ambulance personnel. Mother is in excruciating pain—crying. Forty-five minutes later, the doctor arrives. Thirty minutes later, they finally do the x-ray. Thirty minutes after that, they get me from the waiting room.

Mother is nowhere in sight. The doctor proceeds to question why Mother did not have her hip repaired. He tells me that it is too late now. I go over all the reasons that I have gone over with other doctors before. Once again, a doctor jumps down my throat, accuses me of writing Mother's death sentence, and wanting her to suffer. Once again, I lose it and tell him to get out of my life and my mother's life.

All the nursing home wants to know is if Mother is able to sit for brief periods of time. The doctor tells me that this will probably be okay in a month or so. I ask him where she is. He sends me down the hallway to a room. She is sitting in a wheelchair screaming and crying in pain. I find a nurse and just lose it!

Of course, there is no doctor to be found, and they tell me there is nowhere for Mother to lie down and wait for the ambulance that will transport her to the nursing home. I sit with her for an hour-and-a-half before the ambulance personnel arrive.

They ask me what Mother's problem is. I tell them that she has a broken hip and the doctor does not want her sitting for about a month. One of the ambulance personnel blows sky high, finds the nurse and says that he intends to file a report on the Clinic for cruelty. I am comforted by this.

All I can do by this time is to help Mother get back to the nursing home, settle in, get some pain medication, and go home. When you see your mother handled like a piece of meat and abused by medical personnel who accuse you of writing her death sentence, it leaves a lasting impression.

FOR THE REMAINDER OF OCTOBER, THERE IS A BREAK IN MY JOURNAL. I am convinced at this point that there is no reason to continue writing. I am just repeating man's inhumanity to man over and over to no avail. The problems are not going away, and my energy in writing seems wasted.

November 1995

Mother is moved to the first floor of Meadow Brook. I walk down the hall the first afternoon of her move. As I turn the corner of the nurses' station in search of her new room, one of the nurses stops me. "Are you looking for your mother?" I reply that I am. The nurse says, "You just walked by her."

I turn around and have my first experience with nursing home living in general.

In the Dining Hall, which is the common area, there is a host of people—including my mother. She is sitting in a Gerri chair. I look at her and at the other residents. I am horrified. She looks just like everyone else here.

For the first time since all of this has transpired, I realize that Mother is no different from the rest. I almost want to vomit. I cannot believe that this person in this chair is my mother. Just four months ago, she was an active human being. Now, she is reduced to a vegetable status in this place. I push these feelings aside and greet her with excitement.

I tell her how great it is to see her up and how much fun it will now be for her since she will be able to be with other people instead of staying cooped up in her room all the time. Mother does not care what I am saying. She is hurting, agitated, and wants to go to bed.

I get the nurse, and we take Mother to her room. I am glad to be in her space, glad to be rid of all those other people and the sights and sounds of the reality of Meadow Brook. I just do not know if I can take this. What has become of the elegant, genteel Southern Lady that I called my mother? What has become of me? It all seems lost. And, it is.

November 3, 1995

ALL MY JOURNAL INDICATES ON THIS DAY is that Mother is hurt.

November 6, 1995

I talk with the nurse practitioner today. She is going to put Mother back on Ativan two times daily for agitation. She is also going to begin restraining Mother in her bed for safety. The last two weeks, her mornings have been pretty good according to the records, but in the afternoon and early evening, she is extremely aggressive.

November 10, 1995

Padding has been put on the rails of Mother's bed to prevent her from hurting her arms when she tries to get out of bed. When I arrive at Meadow Brook, she is trying to get out of the bed—her feet and legs to her knees are off the foot of the bed. She cannot see over the pads on the rails. She is trying to get the pads off. I lower the pads on the bar on the rails so that she can see over them. That seems to help. I wonder why no one thought of this? I get Mother back up in the bed, as the restraint is tight around her chest. Again, through the week, her morning behavior is recorded as good; afternoons she continues to be extremely agitated and aggressive.

November 17, 1995

I arrive at Meadow Brook at 3:30 p.m. Mother is fighting, cursing, and hitting herself. I requested medication for her. The nurse brought it at 4 p.m. Mother will not take it. I ask for the PRN shot to be given. The nurse said they did not have the shot medication available. The nurse promises that she will get her calmed down and give her an Ativan pill. I know Mother is not going to calm down anytime soon, but I have to leave. Let the records show that no medication is charted for her after I leave on this day. This to me is cruel and unusual punishment for someone who cannot control themselves.

November 18, 1995

I arrive at Meadow Brook at 10 a.m. Mother is getting up. She is now able to be in a wheelchair. She enjoys being in her chair, visiting with other ladies in the Dining Hall and eating meals with them.

I give her a manicure—scraping BM from under her nails. This has become a weekly routine for us; otherwise, her nails are not cleaned.

We have lunch together. Mother is put back in bed at 1 p.m. She is given Ativan at 1:15 p.m. She sleeps fifteen minutes and wakes up for about thirty minutes. This is a cycle she has developed in the afternoons. When awake, she is extremely agitated. This cycle continues throughout the entire afternoon until the staff get her out of bed. She is calm for a few minutes and then becomes even more agitated.

November 19, 1995

I arrive at Meadow Brook at 10:15 a.m. Mother is up in the dining hall visiting with her friends. We eat lunch together. She goes back to bed at 12:30 p.m. She sleeps ten minutes. Agitation begins. She fights to get out of bed but does not want to get back in her wheelchair.

The nurse brings Ativan at 2 p.m. Mother is so agitated that she will not take the pill. The nurse tries again, but Mother still refuses to take it. I ask for the PRN shot to be given, but the nurse tells me that it is still not available. I cannot believe that medication is prescribed and yet is never available when it is needed.

Mother is given a shot of something at 3:30 p.m. It takes three of us to hold her down to give her the shot. I leave for fifteen minutes to gain my composure.

I go back at 4 p.m. Mother is beginning to calm down—falling asleep. Obviously, the dosage of Ativan they have prescribed for her is not working.

Before taking her off medications in October, Mother did not have to be restrained. She hates being restrained. At least twenty to twenty-one hours of her day is spent in bed. I understand the safety factor, but better monitoring and better medication control could make a difference.

As POA, I am asking that more medication be given to lesson restraint time. Perhaps it is time to change her medication and try a different drug. Ativan seems to be sending her bouncing off the ceiling most of the time now. It is less than humane to tie someone in a bed and let them fight for hours like an animal when medication is available to calm them down. Of course, medication has to be available and given at the appropriate times for it to be effective! And the fight goes on to give Mother peace.

The upcoming Thanksgiving holiday finds me depressed. Nothing changes with Mother—it just remains a constant day-to-day battle that I have to face. It is so hard to do this alone. I wish my family would take an active part in her care so that some of my load could be lightened. I have been told that John visits some mornings. I do not know when or how many. I never see or hear from him. They never call. It is a long road to walk alone. I wish John and his family knew how alone I feel. I wish it seemed that they care. I wish someone knew and cared.

Thanksgiving Day, November 23, 1995

John did call last night to ask me to eat Thanksgiving lunch with them. I informed him that I would be having Thanksgiving lunch with Mother. That was my place. I am not sure he was very pleased with my decision, but I do not care. This is probably the last Thanksgiving that I will spend with my mother, and I plan to make it as easy as possible for her.

I arrive at Meadow Brook at 10 a.m. I fix her hair and give her a manicure before lunch. Mother seems to enjoy this. She does not have a roommate at this time and by lunchtime is tired. She chooses to eat lunch in her room.

At 12 p.m., lunch is brought. I fix Mother's tray and mine and begin to eat and to help her eat. In walks John and his family. She is so glad to see them. I ask John to help feed Mother while I finish my lunch. He does.

After lunch, Mother wants to get up. John and his family leave the room while I get her up. We take her to the living room. Mother wants family pictures made. Will leaves to go and buy a disposable camera for us. When he returns, we have one of the CNAs take our family pictures.

Mother begins to get agitated, and the family leaves. I put her back to bed and request that her medication be given. She takes it and falls asleep. I quickly leave. This is an emotional time for me, and I have taken all that I can for one day. I do not want to be here through the afternoon to endure the sleep-agitation-sleep cycle. I know that it will happen—it always does these days. I just need to go home and cry. And, I do.

November 24, 1995

It is the day after Thanksgiving. I go to Meadow Brook very early. I have breakfast with Mother, settle her in bed for her morning nap, and go home. I cannot cope with Meadow Brook today. I do not go back on this day.

Upon returning home, my anger bursts forth. I want life to return as it was and yet know that it never will. I decide to move my bedroom into my mother's room where I may feel comfort from the way it was. To this end, I first remove everything from her closet and pile it on my bed in my room. I go to a local store and buy new closet shelving to redo her closet to suit the needs of my clothes. My minister, Allen, comes down and helps me install the rods and the shelving. By the time he arrives, I have ripped up the carpet in her room about halfway.

My anger is such that I need to tear up something. And tear I do!! After Allen helps me complete the closet project and leaves, I finish tearing the carpet out of the room. There are beautiful hardwood floors underneath. Maybe this will be a sign that things will get better. I doubt it, but I keep on tearing. I work until midnight, and my new room is finished. Mother's room is now mine. My clothes are in her closet. It is now my closet. I am using her furniture that I have always loved—but the rest is now mine.

I take a shower and prepare to go to bed. As I crawl beneath the sheets, I realize that I have not changed them. They are my mother's. Her scent is on them. I feel her close to me. I cry. I cry. And, I cry more. I sleep.

THIS IS THE BEGINNING OF "HOME IMPROVEMENTS" for me. I have this strong urge to "make this house my own." My anger is real for the circumstances surrounding my life and the life of my mother. I need to begin to replace the old with the different. The old life is gone. I know that. And this great urge to cleanse myself of the old is compelling.

I spend the next two months and all my savings converting *our* house to *my* house. I need to go slower. But the storm in my life will not let me. I am raging against the fury of the wind and the rain, and all I can do is run, and run, and run. The more I can change, the further away I feel from the storm. And believe me, the storm rages.

This is only the beginning. I am only two months into nursing home life and already feel lost and ready to give up. Why must people suffer as my mother is suffering now? Where are all the people in my life whom I always thought would be there for us? The storm rages.

After the pictures were developed from our "family" Thanksgiving. I take them for Mother to see. She looks very carefully at each picture. In each picture, she is the focal point as we are all standing around her in her wheelchair. After carefully looking at each one, Mother looks up and asks, "I wonder where I was and why I am not in the pictures?" I could have cried. Mother did not recognize herself in a single picture.

Where has my mother gone? She must be further away from me than I realize. I look very lovingly at her and reply, "Oh, you were there, Mother. You must have been taking the pictures. But, believe me, Mother, you were there!!" I do not know how I thought to say that, but I will always remember it. As I look at one of the pictures that I have placed on my desk, an interesting feature strikes me. As we are all gathered around Mother as a family, there are only two people in the picture touching another person. They are Will and me. I think this says a lot about our family and the bond that we truly share. Or, at least it does to me. I thank God for Will and the love he so openly expresses to me and to his grandmother.

There is another break in my journal at this point until December 2nd. Emotionally, I am just too tired to try and write anymore. And, as in October, I find that I am seeing the same things over and over and over again.

December 1995
Saturday, December 2, 1995

After lunch, Mother goes to bed, extremely sweet on this day. She wants to talk after getting in bed. I take this opportunity to ask her what she wants to give her family and close friends for Christmas. She thinks for a long time and finally says, "Whatever I give, I want to make sure that my family will always remember me as I was, not like this. And, I want them to always know how much I love them." I promise her that I will fulfill both of those requests. I could just lay down with her and cry right now.

I let Mother fall asleep, and then I leave to find the gifts to fulfill her wishes. As I am driving home, I think of a beautiful picture I have of her. If I have that copied and framed, it will fulfill her first request. When I get home, I get the one copy I have of the picture of her and take it to a local camera store to get it copied. They refuse to copy the picture due to copyright laws.

I explain my situation to them, but to no avail. There is no mention anywhere on Mother's picture as to what photography studio took the picture, so I cannot obtain their permission to have it copied. I leave the camera store crying.

At a photography studio on my way back home, I find a way to have it copied. It takes much ingenuity, not to mention two angels on Earth who help me with my plight, but I am able to have the picture copied, purchase frames for each one, and thus, fulfill Mother's first request to "always remember me as I was."

Mother has always been an avid reader. To fulfill her second request, I try and think of a book I can buy each member of our family that would convey her love to them. I go to a local bookstore and begin to look on the new releases shelf. The book, The Christmas Box by Richard Paul Evans seems to jump off the shelf into my hands. In the new releases area, there is a sofa in front of a warm fireplace. I sit down and quickly read the book. The tears fall from my eyes as I realize that I have found the answer to Mother's second request. The Christmas Box is a gift of healing that I needed so desperately. For the first time, walking this journey with Mother, thanks to Richard and his words of healing through his book, I find joy deep within my heart. I purchase all the copies they have in the store. I then go to another bookstore and buy Christmas Love boxes to go with each book. I have fulfilled both of Mother's requests and will now pass on through her, the gift of healing for us all!

Sunday, December 3, 1995

I take all of the books I have purchased to Meadow Brook. Mother is sitting up in her chair in her room. She spends the next two hours painstakingly writing a message in each book for the special people in her life. I nearly lose it emotionally so many times as she writes from her heart. It is so hard for her to write now. But, write she does.

I know, somehow in my heart that this will be our last Christmas and Mother, unknowingly, is making it special for all those she loves. Well, I say unknowingly, but maybe in her own heart, she does know. Who is to say?

Tuesday, December 5, 1995

When I am ready to leave for the day, a nurse comes and tells me that Mother has a bruise on her back. Another nurse had called my house during the day and left a message on my answering machine. I thank the nurse for telling me and go home. I am used to bruises on Mother and am not alarmed.

Wednesday, December 6, 1995

When preparing to change Mother, I see the bruise on her back. There is some bruising on her lower back above waist level. This in itself is not alarming. What is alarming is what appears to be a rope burn across her back at the same point

I ask for a nurse to look at it because it is inflamed and oozing. The nurse puts a bandage on it. I inquire as to how it happened. I am told that it must have come from the restraint belt when Mother was struggling to get it off. Why had someone not seen the inflammation or oozing before I called it to their attention? And this is a good nursing home.

During the night, I am called by the nurse to let me know that Mother scraped her right arm while the CNA was putting her to bed. Goodnight.

Thursday, December 7, 1995

While I am visiting Mother, the nurse changes the bandage on her right arm. It is much worse than a scrape. What did Mother scrape her arm on? No one seems to know. So, what else is new? I talk to the social worker, Kay, and ask her to try and find out how Mother has been hurt—both the rope burn and the scrape. She says that she will find out.

Saturday, December 16, 1995

This is another "gift day." I arrive in the morning. Christmas music is playing in the dining hall. Mother is sitting with her friends, and we all have a grand time making a Christmas list for family and friends. Mother actually writes some of the items herself. I will cherish the copy of that list forever. She also makes a notation at the top of one of the pages that says, "Life certainly would have been dull without Nancy."

Indeed, I cherish that statement—Mother actually knows who I am today. She is having such a good time, and I am, too. There are some redeeming moments in life at Meadow Brook that bring joy to the journey.

Mother begins to get a little agitated by this time. I ask her how she feels and she replies, "Fine as a frog's hair split thirteen ways." I write that down so I will never forget it!

As we wait to have our lunch trays brought to our table, I ask her what she wants. She keeps saying, "I want . . . I want . . . I want." She finally says that she wants a fifth of liquor. I ask her if that is what she wants for Christmas. Mother screams, "Hell no, I want it now!" For a lady who does not curse nor drink, that is quite a statement and quite a scene that will replay itself in my mind forever. A moment in time that will always bring a smile to my face, a chuckle to my heart. A moment that, indeed, brought a little joy to this journey.

The mind plays so many tricks on the people suffering from Alzheimer's. You just have to accept most things in the humor in which they sometimes present themselves. This same day, a lady who always rolls her wheelchair around and around screaming, "God help me" over and over really agitates Mother to the breaking point. She finally looks at the lady and says, "Why don't you call on someone who knows you?" I guess at this time, Mother probably feels that God has abandoned all of the people here—I certainly do—including myself. But, in my heart, and I suppose in her heart, too, it is not true. It is just a human thought in the midst of the storm.

Tuesday, December 19, 1995

I have the shock of my life. It is 5:15 p.m. I am at home and have the answering machine on while I am getting dressed to go to Bill and Peggy's (my cousin's home) for a family dinner with Erwin (my cousin). Mother calls. She is extremely agitated and wanting to come home.

I just let the machine pick up the message. I cannot deal with that tonight. At 6 p.m., Carolyn calls. Mother called their house and talked with Will. She was very agitated and wanted a ride home. Carolyn wants to know what to do. I tell her to either ignore the call or go to Meadow Brook and check on Mother. She chooses to ignore the call and does not go and check on her.

I have a wonderful time at Bill and Peggy's. Erwin comes, and we celebrate Christmas together.

When I arrive back home at 10:45, there are two messages on my answering machine from the nurse at Meadow Brook. Mother has fallen out of her wheelchair in her room. I call and talk with the nurse. Mother is now in bed asleep and seems okay.

Wednesday, December 20, 1995

I arrive at Meadow Brook at 7:30 a.m. Mother is just waking up. I meet the nurse on her way in. She is very apologetic about Mother falling out of her chair. I ask if Mother was wearing her restraint. She says, "Oh, yes." "Was she agitated?" I ask. "No," replies the nurse.

I check the behavior chart and see that nothing is charted. The nurse comes to Mother's room. I ask again how she could fall out of her chair with her restraint on, particularly if she were not agitated? "The ties come off easily," is her reply. My other question is why was Mother was left in her room in her chair alone with no supervision? A CNA later tells me that Mother had been so agitated they rolled her back in her room hoping that this would calm her down.

None of the explanations make sense—but all have to be accepted. There is no one who will really tell you the truth about incidences such as this. Mother's knee is swollen. The nurse looks at the knee.

Mother has breakfast. I leave at 9:30 a.m. I return around 3:15 p.m. My longtime friend, Sheila, goes with me. Mother is in her room with two staff members. She is extremely agitated. She has a new roommate in the room with two family members and two children. Mother is yelling and fighting. Upon seeing me, the CNAs leave the room, telling me, "See if you can do anything with her."

Mother continues to yell and claws my neck, drawing blood. I go to the nurses' station, leaving Sheila to watch Mother. I ask the nurse if they have any idea what is going on with Mother. I ask for a shot to be given to her to help calm her down. I ask the CNA to put her to bed. They do and give her a shot.

I leave the room again at 3:25. Sheila goes with me to the nurses' station. I talk with the nurse practitioner regarding agitation, the fall, medications, and Mother's knee. I talk with the social worker, Kay. My concerns are how did Mother fall if restrained and not agitated? Two phone calls to the family document the agitation, behaviors not charted honestly, therefore medication cannot be monitored effectively. Why is a shot not given for agitation?

If agitation for Mother means that she hurts herself, why are we allowing her to do this? Last, but not least, what is the plan of action if she refuses medication? I ask the nurse practitioner to look at her knee.

Sheila and I leave Meadow Brook. I call back at 5:20 p.m. The nurse practitioner has not yet been down to see Mother. She goes and then calls me back. She asked Mother if she had been going to the bathroom frequently. Mother tells her that she does void frequently but does not have any burning sensation. The nurse practitioner orders an in/out catheter to rule out kidney infection. She did not look at Mother's knee. I asked her to go back and look at her knee and to call me back. She does.

She tells me Mother's knee is swollen from arthritis, that she has no problem with range of motion. Why in God's name do people ask and accept answers from people suffering from Alzheimer's? And why was Mother's knee not swollen before she had fallen if it is due to arthritis?

Our minister of music visited Mother on Tuesday afternoon and reported to me that Mother was very agitated, to the point of trying to hit him. Why does everyone keep reporting to me that this is not happening? Would it not be better for all concerned just to be honest? That way, proper medication could be given which would in all probability give Mother a little peace. Why are we so cruel to those who need us the most?

Thursday, December 21, 1995

I arrive at Meadow Brook at 9:30 a.m. Mother is in bed, very agitated, soaking wet, no diaper, no blanket or afghan. Everything is soaked and smells horrid!

I talk with the social worker, Kay. Mother is given a shower, and her bed is changed. I leave at 11:15 a.m. and return at 12:45 p.m. I help Mother finish her lunch. I take her to a Christmas program. Mother sings every word of every Christmas song with me. I could cry.

I take her back to her room and put her in bed at 3 p.m. I change her. Mother is a little agitated, but I know that she is tired. What a great time we have had together today. I play her music box for her. She is going to sleep. Ativan is given at 3 p.m. I notice that there is no change in the dosage as discussed with me by the nurse practitioner. I inquire, but no one seems to know that there is to be a change. They check Mothers' chart and an extra amount is given as should have been. I really should be on the payroll at Meadow Brook.

The dietitian comes and talks with me at my request regarding Mother's weight loss. She orders milkshakes between meals and potatoes with meals to give extra calories. I leave at 4 p.m.

Friday, December 22, 1995

I arrive at Meadow Brook at 10 a.m. Mother is in bed. The CNA comes and bathes her, changes her, and puts her in her wheelchair. Mother's restraint is not put on.

I stay and have lunch with Mother. I put her back in bed after lunch. I inform the nursing staff that Mother's restraint is not on. No one can find it. The social worker, Kay, gets a new one. She asks the CNA to put it on. Mother is slightly agitated, but I am able to calm her by sitting with her and playing her music box.

I leave at 1:15 p.m. On my way down the hall to leave, a nurse stops me and informs me that they feel Mother might have pneumonia. They want to begin giving her antibiotics. I simply stare at her. This is one of the moments I have dreaded. I am now the one to tell her not to give antibiotics to Mother if she has pneumonia. I know that this will be writing a death sentence for Mother, but it is what she would want. It is still so very hard to say. But I do.

I get in my car and burst into tears. Have I just given permission for Mother to die? "Dear Lord, please do not let Mother die at Christmas. My heart could not take it." In my head also are thoughts of relief—thoughts that all of this could finally be coming to an end for Mother and for me. "But, God, please not at Christmas." It is amazing to me how the things we want the most, we only want at a time convenient for ourselves.

Saturday, December 23, 1995

When I arrive at Meadow Brook, my new deacon and his wife (Chet and Sue) are visiting with Mother. I requested a new deacon after the escapade we had while Mother was in the hospital. They seem to have had a good visit with Mother.

As I walk them to the door to leave, they ask me if there is anything they can do for me. I say, " I just wish I could have a day off." They ask me to call them sometime, and they would arrange that for me. I said that I would.

I give Mother a manicure. She is very tired and very congested. I take her to the second floor for restorative feeding. She is too tired to stay. I take her back to her room and put her in bed. She sleeps twenty minutes until her lunch comes.

I feed her—she eats very little but does drink her tea. I leave so that she can get some sleep. I arrive back at 2:30 p.m. The CNA is changing her. I get Mother up and fix her hair. Erwin, her nephew, comes by for a visit. Mother goes back to bed. She does use the bedpan for me. I do not understand why the staff cannot get her to use it for them. I really do not believe that they try.

Mother is still very congested. The nurse confronts me again about the use of antibiotics. I tell her again not to administer any antibiotics unless I am consulted first. Mother has been calm all day.

Christmas Eve, December 24, 1995

I arrive at Meadow Brook at 10 a.m. Mother is up and stays up until 10:30 a.m. She is very tired. She goes back to bed and sleeps through two visitors. I am able to get her to eat sherbet and drink tea and water for lunch. She goes back to sleep.

She wakes up at 2 p.m. when the family comes to visit. I leave at 3 p.m. and return at 4 p.m. Mother has just gotten up. We share Christmas Eve dinner in the dining hall. Mother eats a good dinner.

While in the dining hall, a young couple comes in with their two little children. They have brought every resident a Christmas bag. I talk with them. It seems that one day they were riding by Meadow Brook and wondered what it was? They stopped to inquire. They decided to do this as their Christmas gift to their family. What a wonderful way to speak of the true meaning of Christmas for all!

Mother goes back to bed at 6:30 p.m. I leave at 6:45 p.m. She has been calm all evening—keeps saying that she wants to go home for Christmas. On my way home, I cry thinking of the Silent Night where all is calm, all is bright. Will it ever be again for me? I want Mother to be able to come home, but I know this is not possible. All is calm, and on this Christmas Eve night in our lives, all was made a little brighter by an unknown family who gave of their love to people who so desperately need it—including me. For another moment in time at Meadow Brook, I, along with our Meadow Brook family, found joy in the journey.

Christmas Day, December 25, 1995

I PREFACE THIS ENTRY BY SAYING THAT JOHN CALLED ME Christmas Eve wanting to know what time I was coming to their house Christmas morning. I explained to him that I was not—that I was going to share Christmas with Mother at Meadow Brook—and suggested that they might want to do that, too. Reception of that idea was not taken well. I know that they cannot understand my commitment to Mother and to seeing that her needs are met, but all I can say is if they are ever in Mother's position, I hope there will be someone who will go the extra mile to help them. Someone must be there, and I have chosen to be that someone. I gave up on getting help months ago. Oh, I still wish that it would be offered though I know that it will not. Or if it is offered, the offer usually will not be carried through. Something will always come up that will prevent it. That is the pattern. Thus, I choose to spend Christmas with Mother.

I arrive at Meadow Brook at 9:15 a.m. Mother is still in bed. She remains very congested. I help her open her Christmas presents. I have gotten her some new gowns and a bottle of her favorite perfume. She takes a nap until 11 a.m.

Ray and Joyce Deaton come to see her. John and his family come at 11:15 a.m. They open presents with her. Mother becomes slightly agitated—too much confusion for her.

Lunch comes. John and his family leave. I eat in the room with Mother. Joyce helps feed her. Ray and Joyce leave at 12:45 p.m. after opening presents with Mother.

She uses the bedpan for me. Mother has stayed dry the whole time I am with her today. I wish the staff would do this with her, too. After all, it is in her Care Plan, which means it is written down on paper and put in her chart to look impressive. It certainly does not mean that the written plans are ever carried through with on a daily basis.

Mother was mostly calm today—just too much confusion for her. She was able to regain calm after all visitors left. Merry Christmas, Mother.

I leave Meadow Brook and go home and cry most of the afternoon. I am alone for the first time on Christmas Day. My friend, Sheila, and her family took me in Christmas Eve, and I am going over there later today. Without them, I probably would not have been able to stand the feeling of being alone brought on mostly by the abandonment of my family.

It is a hard road to travel, but to travel it alone is almost unbearable. God give me the strength to continue the journey with my mother!

December 26, 1995

I arrive at Meadow Brook at 9:30 a.m. Mother is in her chair in her room. She is agitated. She will not take medication from me, the nurse, or the social worker, Kay. I finally get her to take it by putting her back in bed. Sometimes the obvious is the most simple.

Mother eats a good lunch and then naps. I leave around 1 p.m.

December 27, 1995

I arrive at Meadow Brook around 11 a.m. Mother is in her room in her chair. The lights are off, and the curtains are drawn. A magazine is on her lap. She is asleep. Again, why would anyone leave a person in a dark room by themselves? The magazine is a nice touch, but how can she see it in the dark? I guess I would just go to sleep, too.

The Director of Nursing comes and talks with me about giving Mother antibiotics. I explain that we do not want to treat pneumonia with antibiotics. She tells me that they have discovered that she has a urinary tract infection and if this is left untreated, it will be very painful for Mother. I fall for her trap and agree to give Mother antibiotics. The thought of her being in pain is more than my heart can bear at this time.

THERE IS ANOTHER BREAK IN MY JOURNAL AT THIS POINT. New Year's Eve is particularly hard on me. I realize that the New Year is going to bring only part of the Old Year to my life, and I am not sure that I can cope much longer with anything.

Following New Year's will be my birthday—and that is the pits. I don't even mention it to Mother, although I have two books that she has written messages in at Christmas, which are her birthday presents to me. I take those out and have my own personal, one-on-one birthday party the evening of my birthday.

Some things you never forget. And, so the days wear on at Meadow Brook. A broken record of sorts, or so it seems. My next entry on February 12, 1996, says it all. Things do not change at Meadow Brook. I just keep on keeping on, every day, going over and over the same things, trying to get it right for Mother, trying to bring some peace and quality to what life she has left to live.

February 1996
February 12, 1996

I talk with the social worker, Kay, and the Director of Meadow Brook regarding my concerns. They are going to address these with the Director of Nursing and the nursing staff and try to make things better for Mother. I feel better having talked with them. They are so nice and seem to really care about the residents. All the staff are that way. I guess that is why it is so hard to understand the lack of simple everyday care for them. Love is great. Everyone here needs it. But care is a part of that love. Let's see how much good all of this does.

February 13 to February 16, 1996

On Tuesday, Mother's teeth are filthy when I arrive, and she had no bedspread on her bed.

Wednesday, the same with the addition of a hot milkshake sitting on her food tray unopened—no one had helped her drink it.

Thursday, her teeth are filthy again, no bedspread, and her peaches are sitting unopened on her food tray.

Friday, she is soaking wet, trying to get up, no lights on, no bedspread, no diaper. Does this ever end? Maybe we should blow this place up and start over. Some days I feel like it. And, remember, this is a good nursing home.

Saturday, February 17, 1996

Today is Mother's birthday. I am trying hard to make this a good day for her. I pick up a couple of cakes at the grocery store, a balloon to put on her wheelchair in the dining hall, and take her gift to Meadow Brook.

I arrive at 11 a.m. She is sitting in the dining hall talking with Suzanne, my friend. While I am shocked, my heart is so happy to see her. She has loved Mother dearly for many years and continues to share that love with her! She has brought Mother some beautiful flowers for her birthday. She sits holding her hands and talking with her about all the good times they have shared. Mother has the sweetest smile on her face as they talk! I will never forget this beautiful testimony from Suzanne to my mother of her love. I leave the cakes at the nursing station and take Mother her balloon and gift.

Suzanne and I have a good time visiting with Mother. The expression on Mother's face seems to indicate that she understands it is her birthday. Suzanne has to leave. I walk her out, hug her, and let her know how much this day with her has meant to me! I eat lunch with Mother, and we share cake with all of the other residents who can have some.

Joyce, Ray, and Aunt Mabel come to visit. Mother is up longer than usual and becomes slightly agitated. They realize she is tired and leave. I help her back to bed and change her. I wait with her for the nurse to bring her medication. She brings it two hours late. Why? What is the problem? Does it take an act of Congress to get things right?

Anyway, all in all, it is a good day for Mother. I am not really sure how much she understands about this, her special day, but I feel good for sharing it with her. As with every special day, I leave, get in my car, and cry all the way home. Last birthdays are tough. Last birthdays in a nursing home are unbearable!

Sunday, February 18, 1996

When I arrive, I find Mother slumped down in her chair. The restraint is too tight across her chest. There is no bedspread on her bed. There is BM caked under her fingernails.

She has ice tea for lunch, and the doctor has written specific orders for her not to have it. For some reason, they feel this may be adding to her agitation. I give Mother a manicure, have lunch with her, get her an extra blanket for her bed so she will not be cold, help her back to bed, and stay with her until late meds are given and then come home. As the old saying goes, "Same S**t. Different day."

Tuesday, February 27, 1996

Mother is at lunch when I arrive. She is not wearing a bib, and no assistance is being given to help her eat. Her hands are trembling. She is dropping food everywhere. What does it take to get people to see and to help? And they wonder why Mother is losing weight?

Wednesday, February 28, 1996

Two staff members tell me on the way in that Mother is extremely agitated. She is in her room in her chair. She has taken her robe off and is trying to get her gown off. I ask her what she wants. She says that she needs to go to the bathroom. I ring the call bell for help.

The CNA comes and puts her on the commode. She leaves Mother urinating. I stand in the hall trying to get some help. Mother is trying to get up by herself. I cannot leave her. While waiting, I keep smelling a strong odor of urine. Upon inspection, I discover Mother's diaper pad in her chair, her gown, her robe, and pillow at the back of her chair are soaking wet. Is there any wonder she was trying to strip?

I change her gown and her robe. The CNA finally comes and helps Mother get back in her chair. After using the bathroom and being freshened, Mother is okay. Is it any wonder nursing homes get a bad reputation? Why can people not be taken to the bathroom on a more regular basis rather than to be left to wet all over themselves?

There is so much downtime observed which could be put to better use by the staff. The nurse comes to tell me that they did try to brush Mother's teeth after lunch, but that she would not let them. I can believe this—but did anyone try at a later hour? Sometimes five minutes after a refusal of something, Mother can be talked into the very thing that she refused. Granted, sometimes not, but did they try?

I leave at 4:15 p.m. Mother is back in the dining hall looking at the paper calmly. At this point, I have learned that it is easy for me to leave Mother in the dining hall by telling her that I have to go to my computer class. Education was so important to her, and she never minds when I have to go when I tell her this.

We always end these visits with a hug, and I say, "Mother, do you know how much I love you?" She replies, "Yes, a bushel and a peck and a hug around the neck." I say, "What else?" Mother asks, "What?" I reply, "And a smile." And it is her smile that I will always remember.

When I get to the hallway before leaving, I always turn around, look at her beautiful smile, blow her a kiss, and she, in turn, blows one to me. In the midst of the storm, the love we feel for each other abounds even under the worst of circumstances. These are always the moments I will remember about Meadow Brook for these are the moments that are real.

I go back to Meadow Brook on Wednesday evening. There is still no bedspread on her bed. Mother is agitated and will not eat. The CNA is trying to force feed her. I ask her to back off and give Mother some space. Trying to force food into her mouth is only making the situation worse. I put her back to bed and am able to calm her down. The night nurse is able to get her to drink a milkshake. The food log says she ate 50 percent of her meal. What a joke.

Thursday, February 29, 1996

I arrive at Meadow Brook at 4 p.m. Mother's dentures are caked with food. I had put a piece of Kleenex in her denture cup the day before to see if they were using it at all. Needless to say, it is still there. Nothing is new—all grows older—and I grow wearier as I try to make things right for Mother. I surely wish there was someone to help. It may be time for yet another letter and a conference with someone. We will see. I just need to go home and get some rest. I feel like I am ready to cave in.

March 1 to March 31, 1996
March 1, 1996

The days pass quickly, but to me, they are an eternity. Is there no end to this madness? Mother is in such torment and seems to be getting worse each week. I still cannot understand why more medication cannot be given to her. It is a fight I will continue.

I arrive at Meadow Brook at 2:45 p.m. I am early today. I decide to come in the front door. Sometimes the element of surprise is good in a nursing home.

As I come through the living room, I hear Mother screaming for Georgia. Her room is the third room from the living room. As I turn the corner into her doorway, her curtain is pulled. I cannot see her.

I find her halfway down in the bed. Her restraint is extremely tight under her arms and around her chest. She is now softly screaming, "Georgia, help me! It's too tight. I cannot breathe." I immediately pull her up in her bed. My feelings explode with anger. Are these people crazy? Are they going to let this damn restraint choke the life out of my mother? These and other thoughts go through my mind. Mother's diaper is on the floor.

BM is smeared on her pad and her gown. Her sheet is on the floor. I go to get washcloths, towels, pad, sheets, and a diaper. A CNA comes down the hall. She asks me if everything is okay. I say emphatically, "No" and proceed down the hall. She follows me. She helps me clean Mother and the bed.

I ask her how often they check on Mother. The CNA tells me once every two hours. She explains that they must keep the curtain pulled because Mother takes her clothes off; thus, they are not always able to see her when walking down the hall.

At this point, Mother says that she needs to void. The CNA tells her to go ahead, and she will clean her when she is finished. My mind explodes again with anger. Someone just told my mother to use the bathroom in the bed? My God in heaven, where is the dignity in all of this? No one uses the bathroom in the bed intentionally.

I get Mother a bedpan. She uses it. I get her up. I stay until 3:45 p.m. I leave her in the dining hall. I do have someone fasten her restraint before I leave. I schedule a conference with Kay, the social worker for the next day. Enough is enough, and today is inexcusable! I go home to write yet another letter of concern.

March 2, 1996

I have taken another day off from work to have a conference regarding Mother and issues which are, at this point, life-threatening. I include a copy of my letter of concern, which speaks for itself. Much of the same—some new—all an important part of maintaining dignity for Mother.

CONCERNS REGARDING CARE
March 2, 1996
PATIENT: Mary Ann Howie—Room 2128
After several attempts at communicating my concerns regarding care for my mother, I still find that the following concerns need to be addressed. They are basic care concerns as well as safety issues:

Cleanliness: A. Please clean BM from under fingernails as Mary Ann finger feeds at times; B. Please brush her dentures after meals and put them back in her mouth. Be sure food is swallowed, as she is a mouth breather when sleeping; C. Please put lotion barrier cream on after incontinent episodes; D. Please put a bib on at mealtime to protect her clothing.

Bowel/Bladder Re-Training: A. When taken to the bathroom, please monitor her. She cannot be left alone as she will try to get up by herself; B. Offer her a bedpan if not taking her to the bathroom—do not encourage her wetting herself.

Safety with Restraint:

A. When Mary Ann is in her room in bed, check on her more often than every two hours. She is not able to ring the bell for help. She slides down in the bed, thus pulling her restraint up, causing it to be tight over her chest and under her arms.; B. When Mary Ann is in her room in her chair, check on her more often than every two hours. When she slides down in her chair, her restraint comes up tightly over her chest; C. The restraint needs to be tied to her chair if it is going to be useful

Medical: A. Medication should be given at prescribed times so that effects of medication on behavior can be better monitored; B. Orders from Doctor such as not to give tea with meals but rather to give juice to reduce caffeine intake need to be followed.

Nourishment: A. If snacks between meals are needed to help prevent further weight loss, please help the staff to make sure they are taken; B. Assist with feeding since Mary Ann is having problems getting food in her mouth due to hand tremors.

Room Needs: A. Please put a bedspread on her bed each day; B. Please leave lamps on in her room. She loves light; C. Please leave the radio playing soft music for her.

Thank you for your attention to and communication of all concerns with the staff. If all staff are aware of basic care needs, there is no doubt that these needs will be met. I would like to review these in two weeks to ensure progress is being made in all areas.

After my conference with Kay, I find Mother in the dining hall. She is about halfway through lunch. She does have a bib on. She has tea to drink—once again against doctor's orders. I note this with Kay. The CNA takes Mother to the bathroom. I leave around 12:15 p.m. I am tired.

I am at home with my thoughts. Life is a constant battle at Meadow Brook. I never realized the magnitude of all of the talk I have heard throughout my life regarding nursing homes. I guess no one can until they walk in those shoes. The staff at Meadow Brook do love my mother—they tell her so—they hug her when she lets them. I have seen them cry for and with her and with me. That is one of the only things that keep me going. It is a good nursing home. It is just a full-time job for a caregiver!

Sunday, March 3, 1996

I arrive around 10:45 a.m. Mother is in the dining hall reading the paper. She has long since lost her ability to read but loves the paper each morning. She wants to go to the bathroom and wash her hands before lunch. I take her. I discover BM smeared all over her hands. I clean them and show the towel to the CNA. Great God above, help my mother and give me strength not to slap someone before long.

I eat lunch with her. After lunch, she goes to bed. She has no top sheet. I get one and put it on her bed. I brush her teeth for her. She, once again, has tea to drink for lunch. I leave around 2 p.m.

Monday, March 4, 1996

I arrive around 3:45 p.m. Mother is agitated. She thinks that she is having surgery, and there is no convincing her otherwise. I do not even try. I just tell her that everything will be okay, that she has good doctors and the surgery will be over soon. This seems to work. I leave around 4:30 p.m.

Tuesday, March 5, 1996

I arrive at 3:30 p.m. Mother is extremely agitated; swinging from the rafters would be a better way to put it. The nurse tells me she has only been this way for a few minutes. Kay tells me that Mother has been this way for at least one-and-a-half hours. Another nurse agrees and also says that the 2 p.m. dose of Ativan is not helping. Actually, it seems to be making her more agitated. Kay says that she will talk with the nurse practitioner tomorrow and see if we can have Mother taken off Ativan and kept on Haldol exclusively. Haldol is the only drug which seems to work for her. I leave at 4:15 p.m.

Wednesday, March 6, 1996

I arrive around 4:30 p.m. Mother is in bed and fairly calm. She wants to get up at 4:45 p.m. I ask her if she is dry. She says that she is. Upon checking, I find that she has BM smeared on her leg. I check her diaper. She has BM. I ask the CNA to change her and clean her before getting her up. I wonder if I had not been here if she would have been changed and cleaned? What a silly question.

I take Mother to the dining hall. I leave her looking at a magazine. Kay has left for the day, so I cannot talk with her regarding her conversation with the nurse practitioner and medication.

Thursday, March 7, 1996

I arrive at 3:30 p.m. Mother is in bed struggling to get out, crying out for Georgia. She needs to be changed. The CNA comes in at my request and changes her. We get her up. I take her to the dining hall. She is very agitated—scratching—hitting, etc. I stay until 4 p.m. I have had about all of this that I can take for one day.

Saturday, March 9, 1996

I arrive around 10:15 a.m. Mother is in the dining hall looking at the paper. I stay until 11 a.m.

All appears well. I go home. Today I just cannot bear a meal at Meadow Brook. I need to rest.

Sunday, March 10, 1996

I arrive at 10:30 a.m. I have lunch with Mother. I have to feed her again today. Her dentures have not been cleaned after breakfast. I leave around 12:30 p.m. after putting her back to bed.

There has been a medication change which was supposed to begin on Saturday. I talk with the nurse to make sure she is aware of this. The nurse has no idea that she is supposed to give the 2 p.m. medication at 12:30 p.m. Who runs this place, anyway? I ask her to talk with the nurse practitioner.

Monday, March 11, 1996

Once again, I am taking the day off. I arrive at Meadow Brook at 10 a.m. Mother's dentures are filthy from breakfast. I show them to the nurse. She puts a note on Mother's closet door that her dentures are to be cleaned after each meal. Why in God's name would a note have to be placed anywhere? This should be routine care for each resident.

I have the nurse practitioner paged and have three conversations with her. After these conversations, she decides to increase the 12:30 p.m. Ativan to 1 mg. She feels like this will help Mother sleep more. She refuses to take her off this medication. She says that by sleeping more, Mother will not be tormented.

I still cannot understand why it is so hard to believe that the Ativan drives Mother up a wall. Of course, if it were given at the correct times and the behaviors were monitored accurately, the nurse practitioner might get a different picture. Right now the only honest person in all of this is me. And, of course, the social worker, Kay.

I leave and go by my church to see Allen, my minister. He agrees to meet with me and whoever else to see if there is not some way we can adjust or change Mother's medication to give her some degree of peace. I am an emotional basket case. Why is this so hard to do? Kay spoke with the nurse practitioner last week. I thought we had all of this settled. I thought everyone was in agreement to take Mother off Ativan and give Haldol exclusively. Now, another fight. Does anyone care? It doesn't seem so. Why are we so cruel to those whose quality of life is gone? Why can we not give them dignity through peace even if it means medication?

I go back to Meadow Brook at 1 p.m. The nurse gave the new dosage of Ativan at 12:40 p.m. Mother is in bed, fighting to get up. I calm her, and she rests until 2:30—intermittent sleep versus extreme agitation.

I talk briefly with the nurse practitioner again. I schedule an appointment for 2:30 p.m. tomorrow with her and Kay, and I leave.

I go back at 6:45 p.m. Mother is in bed, trying to get out. Her diaper is full of BM and hanging over the bed rail. She is lying on her pad—BM everywhere and soaking wet. Her restraint is not tied. A fresh pad and washcloth are in the room. The CNA bringing the cart down the hall gives me a diaper.

I clean Mother. I put a fresh gown on her. The CNA comes and ties her restraint. I have Mother take her dentures out and brush them—food is caked on them from her two previous meals. I get her some water to rinse her mouth before she goes to sleep.

I leave at 7:45 p.m. to go home. Mother is still going strong, and I cannot take it anymore. I need to get away to protect my fragile self. But, when you are the only one who apparently cares what is going on—well, I just have to stay and see it through. God help me. I am just not sure that I can go on.

Tuesday, March 12, 1996

I arrive at 1:30 p.m. Mother is in bed, again fighting to get up. I get her up. She is extremely agitated. I sit with her in the lobby to wait for Allen. She recognizes Allen getting out of his car. Some things never cease to amaze me. Mother does not know who I am, but she recognizes other people most of the time. When Allen gets to the living room, we have a brief conversation with Mother. She tells Allen that she is going home—that she is going to have final peace. He asks her if she knows when this will happen. Mother says, "Yes, this Friday afternoon at 3:30." Looking at me, she says, "That would give you time to get here from school."

Chills shake all over me. First of all, I have to guess that Mother means she wants to die—after all, that would be her final peace. And second, she obviously knows me. Oh well, Allen and I have a meeting to go to. Friday will take care of itself, but it is surely spooky.

Allen and I take Mother to the dining hall. We meet with Kay and the nurse practitioner. I had asked John to be there, but so far he has not shown up. After our meeting, I find him sitting in the dining hall with Mother. She is still agitated.

As a result of our meeting, they are increasing another dose of Ativan. Glory, glory, won't they ever understand? Ativan makes Mother crazy! The best I can hope is that an extra dose will knock her out.

The whole problem with the Haldol is that the government regulates how much you can give a person in a nursing home. Mother is taking the limit.

"Get out of my life, Government! Get out of my mother's life. How dare you regulate peace for any person? How dare you torment our lives daily? Is there is no justice in this world? You are not my mother. You are not me. You are not a part of our tormented lives. You are just a bunch of bureaucrats up on a hill someplace making stupid laws which affect the lives of very real people. What in God's name has mankind been reduced to? God save us all from ourselves!"

At this point, I need to submit a letter of concern to Meadow Brook regarding many issues that continue in Mother's daily life. I include a copy of it here.

Letter of Concern to Meadow Brook
Tuesday, March 12, 1996
Meeting Regarding Medication —Basic Care Needs
Resident: Mary Ann Howie—Room 2128
My best attempts at communication are most often in written form. My concerns regarding Mary Ann, my mother, are medical and safety now. I placed her at Meadow Brook September 5, 1995, as she had a broken hip and was suffering from Alzheimer's, and I could no longer care for her at home. I still believe that I made a wise choice, and there are loving and caring people on staff here who assume responsibility for her care in a very loving way. I remain extremely grateful for all those who strive to meet her needs.

Her basic care needs continue to be bathing, dressing, assistance with feeding, keeping her dentures clean, and her mouth free of food, keeping her fingernails and hands clean, changing after incontinent episodes, transfer to and from her chair and

bed, and monitoring medication to control
agitation and to provide her with peace.
These are all basic care items that Mary Ann
is no longer able to do for herself.

Regarding cleanliness, I would like to
speak to three areas: Brushing dentures,
keeping fingernails and hands clean, and
keeping her mouth free of food after eating.
The first time these areas were brought to
your attention was on September 10, 1995.
Yet, just yesterday, following breakfast and
again following dinner, her dentures were
not brushed, and her mouth remained full
of food. This is a safety issue for Mother as
she is a mouth breather when she sleeps.
If a piece of food in her mouth or from her
dentures dislodges into her windpipe, she
could choke to death. A note has been put on
her closet door by the nurse regarding this.
It was placed there yesterday morning, and
yet, last evening it occurred again. We need
to find a way to ensure that this problem is
solved quickly and on a consistent basis.

The third issue is one of keeping Mother's
fingernails and hands clean. She finger-
feeds at times and puts her hands in her
mouth to assist in removal of her dentures
or to help clear food from her mouth. When
BM is under her fingernails or smeared on

her hands, this becomes a health issue. Mary
Ann needs to have her fingernails cleaned
each morning as a part of her bathing routine
and needs her hands to be washed after each
incontinent episode or when she is taken to
the bathroom.

The issue of safety regarding her restraint
directly correlates to medication to control
agitation. Mother has, at this present time,
fairly good mornings. She is usually in the
dining hall looking at the paper with her
friends, and her temperament is usually calm.
Around 12:30 p.m., she begins to break down.
Her Ativan given at 2 p.m. or backed to 1 p.m.
seems to have no effect on her agitation.
Thus, her 4 p.m. Haldol takes longer to work
or does not seem to work at all. Mary Ann,
as a result, fights from 12:30 p.m. until after
her 8 p.m. Ativan is given, after which she
reportedly sleeps through the night. She is
in a constant struggle to get out of bed after
lunch. This means that she scoots down to the
foot of the bed and her restraint is thus pulled
up over her chest and under her arms.

On March 1, 1996, I arrived earlier than
usual and found her more than three-fourths
of the way down in her bed with her restraint
up under her arms and tight across her chest.
She was yelling for Georgia, and these were

her words: "Georgia, please help me. I cannot get my breath. I immediately rang for help to pull her up in bed. I asked the CNA how often they check on her after lunch. The CNA said that they check on her every two hours. She also said that they keep the curtains pulled since Mother tries to take her clothes off. This means that she cannot be seen from the hallway. Let it be noted again that Mary Ann is not able to use her call bell to ask for help.

I have also found her in her chair in her room behind her curtain where she scoots down in the chair, thus pulling the restraint up under her arms, and it becomes tight across her chest. This is of grave concern to me. The solution to her safety is one, I believe, of regulating her medication to the point that she is peaceful and not having to fight. Most days, her words to me are, "Why are you letting me go on being tormented?" I truly believe that the word torment is an accurate statement made by a human being who has just enough cognitive ability left to realize that she is tormented. These are not demented words.

It is of great concern to me as Mother's daughter that you are allowing her to remain "tormented." While we are all providing her basic bodily care needs, you are ignoring her mental needs and thus denying her of her dignity through the last days of her life. Mary Ann deserves peace, and this can be achieved through medication.

Part of the problem is the lack of accurate reporting of Mother's agitation by the nursing staff. Just last week, a day when Mother was extremely agitated, the nurse told me she had only been like that for a few minutes. Kay had observed that she had been agitated for almost two hours. Reports of agitation must be reported accurately to help us help Mother.

To me, what we are doing by depriving her of peace by letting her continue to remain agitated and "fighting" is like depriving a terminally ill cancer patient of morphine to control pain. Why is it that we cannot give her peace through proper medication to control her pain which happens to stem from Alzheimer's? This would not only make her existence a better one but would make her care easier.

Safety issues regarding restraint would not be an issue if Mother were not fighting. Let her have a good morning time up in the dining hall through lunchtime, and let her have peace through the afternoon and evening through medication. I ask that medically we do all we can to ease her pain and maintain her dignity through giving her peace.

It is my hope that a resolution will be reached regarding these issues when we meet at 2:30 p.m. I do this out of love for my mother and out of the conviction that were she able to speak for herself, these would be her words, as well. My gratitude again is for all who care for her and continue to strive with me to administer to her and to meet her basic needs—and most of all, to provide Mother with dignity through peace.

—Nancy Howie

Wednesday, March 13, 1996

Mother is ballistic! It is reported to me by Kay and a nurse that Mother went to get her hair done and came back very agitated. The fire alarm went off, and Mother went ballistic again. It has taken four people to hold her down to give her a shot of Ativan. She has had no lunch. She is in bed.

The CNA helps me get her up, and I feed her a snack. I leave for a few minutes. I cannot take this any longer. When I return to her room, she is one-fourth of the way down in her chair struggling to get out. I pull her back up ad roll her all over Meadow Brook while she screams, shouts, attempts to hit and scratch everyone and everything in sight. I roll her outside for a few minutes. This seems to help somewhat. I bring her back in and get her some orange juice. I leave her in the dining hall around 3:30 p.m. I must get away. I am ready to blow. When I arrive home, there is a message from Kay that they are taking Mother off Ativan. There is a God! I talk with a doctor in the Department of Psychiatry at a local hospital. He has found with older patients with Alzheimer's that there appears to be a paradoxical reaction with Ativan/Haldol combination. The best thing is to take patients off Ativan and increase Haldol to manage agitation. Seems simple enough to me. Have I not been saying this for over a month?

Thursday, March 14, 1996

I arrive at 9:15 a.m. Mother is in the dining hall. She has had some agitation this morning. I eat lunch with her. She enjoys her lunch. I talk again with the nurse practitioner. She is once again changing medication for her. She will give Haldol at 10 a.m., 12:30 p.m., and 4 p.m. She will also give Ativan at 8 a.m. and 8 p.m. Why, why, why? I do not think that anyone understands what is going on but me. And, obviously, no one thinks that I know anything. Maybe I don't. But, I do have common sense.

Friday, March 15, 1996

The nurse reports a little agitation in the morning, but after Mother gets up, she is okay. She eats a good lunch. I asked for her Haldol at 12:30 p.m. The nurse had forgotten she was supposed to have it. She sleeps until 2 p.m. She awakes slightly agitated and wanting to go home. She says she needs to void. I get her bedpan. She uses it. I brush her teeth. Nobody checks on her until 2:45 p.m. We are in her room with the door closed. How does anyone know how she is doing? How do they know that I have not gone home? It continues to amaze me!

Saturday, March 16, 1996

I have lunch with Mother. She is slightly agitated. She sleeps for two hours after lunch. She is calm upon waking. I leave around 3 p.m. She is still in bed. I reminded the CNA to brush her teeth, which now have breakfast and lunch caked on them. Some days, I just cannot do it myself. Of course, that probably means that it does not get done—but I cannot help it.

Sunday, March 17, 1996

I arrive at 10:15 a.m. I give Mother her weekly manicure. I have lunch with her and put her back to bed. She goes to sleep. I reminded the CNA to brush her teeth.

While having lunch today, Mother is unusually quiet. She keeps looking around the dining hall. I ask her if she needs anything. She says, "No, but you do." I say, "Mother, what do I need?" She replies, "You need to find some younger friends to run around with." I reply, "Yes, you are right Mother, and someday I will. But for now, where else could I find all this wit and wisdom?" I know that in Mother's mind, she perceived that I had invited all my friends for Sunday lunch. After looking around, she was right. I did need to find some younger friends! Another redeeming day in the life of Meadow Brook!

Monday, March 18, 1996

I arrive around 3:30 p.m. Mother has visitors. She is very calm in bed. The smell of urine is overbearing. After the visitors leave, I find that she is soaking wet. I call for help to change her and clean her. After changing her, we get her up, and I take her to the dining hall. She is very calm and sweet. The nurse reports several periods of agitation, but Mother has been able to recoup. If only this could continue.

Tuesday through Thursday

Mother has a good week with only a few periods of slight agitation. She even went and had her hair done without incident.

Friday, March 22, 1996

Mother has had a rough night. She was given a shot of Ativan at 3:30 a.m. She is off her medication schedule because of this and is extremely agitated. I do not stay long. This is a day I need my mother— but will not have her. This is my "Nancy Day"—the day that Mother and Daddy adopted me. This has been the most special day of my life every year— even better than birthdays.

Even with Mother agitated, I put the bed rail down and sit beside her on the bed. I hold her hand. She calls me Nancy. She knows me! I begin to cry. I ask her to think back forty-seven years ago to March 22nd to see if she can remember what she was doing.

She thinks for a long time. Suddenly, she says, "Of course, I remember what I was doing. That was one of the most special days of my life. Your daddy and I adopted you. The tears flowed down both of our cheeks as we hugged and loved as in the days of old. Another moment in time where God allowed me to have my mother again and to affirm the love we shared throughout all our lives. Thank you, God, for the little things that bring joy in our journey at Meadow Brook.

Sunday, March 24, 1996

I arrive at 10:15 a.m. I give Mother her weekly manicure. The nurse reports to me that she has a bruise on her hip—probably from trying to get out of bed. A little later, a CNA takes me into the linen room and tells me she discovered the bruise on Mother when she came on for her shift at 7 a.m. She says that I really need to look at it—that something bad has happened to my mother.

We take her to the bathroom—the bruise is very large. I stay until 3:15 p.m. to talk to the second shift people. No one seems to know anything. I get very upset—even cry out of frustration. I tell the nurse that I do not know what happened to my mother, but I intend to find out. I leave in tears.

I want to pick Mother up in my arms and bring her home where she will be safe, but I know I cannot do this. I will take yet another day off on Monday and talk with Kay and the Director of Meadow Brook. I call John, but he cannot come on Monday to meet with us—he is busy.

After lunch, Mother rests until 1:45 p.m. She wants to get up. I drive her around in her wheelchair. I take her outside for a little while. She is slightly agitated but moving around helps. It still amazes me that while she is in bed after lunch, no one checks.

Since she cannot call with the bell, this remains a perfect setup for her to get hurt. How many times do I have to say this?

Monday, March 25, 1996

When I arrive at Meadow Brook, Kay has called Adult Protection Services and pictures have been taken of the massive bruising on Mother's buttocks. An investigation will be done by Meadow Brook and by Social Services.

Tuesday, March 26, 1996

Social Services comes to investigate. They talk with me, and I explain the chain of events. I tell them that my main question is why someone did not call me at home to let me know that Mother was hurt. Every little bruise or skin tear that she has received here, and it has been many, someone has called me immediately, whether I'm at home or at work. Now Mother has a massive bruise, and no one seems to know what happened. I tell them that this just cannot be so. Someone knows. Someone was there. It could have been as simple as dropping her down too hard on the commode or in her chair. But someone knows!

The Assistant Director of Nursing convinces Social Services that Mother had a platelet burst. She noted for them that Mother's platelets were below 37,000 and I have refused to let them transfuse her. This is true. Mother, herself, has always said that she would not do anything if this were the case. I simply honor this for her. Anyway, this has nothing to do with Mother's bruise. But Social Services bought it hook line and sinker! Guess I have lost again. Actually, Mother is the one who has lost. I just hope that whoever did this to her can live with themselves. This is the best that I can do.

Wednesday, March 27, 1996

Mother is slightly agitated. I do not stay long. I am exhausted.

Thursday, March 28, 1996

We sign a Health Care Power of Attorney for Mother, refusing transfusions, any medication that might prolong her life, and the right to refuse food or drink for herself. These are not easy decisions knowing the consequences. But it is the right decision. It is the decision that Mother made herself, long ago. That is what you must carry in your heart. As tormented as Alzheimer's leaves loved ones, there is still a part of you that does not want to give them up, yet you know that they deserve better and you must give them better when circumstances allow you to make better choices for them. But it is tough. When the words finally flow from your mouth and a life or death decision is made, or when it is put in writing—it is tough.

The amazing thing about this day was that Mother knew the three people who came to draw up her Health Care Power of Attorney, and she stated in her own words what she wanted. Go figure. Without her expressing her awareness of this legal matter we would not have been able to complete her new Health Care Power of Attorney. Thanks be to our Awesome God for giving us this brief moment in time!

April 1 to April 26, 1996
Monday, April 1, 1996

I arrive at Meadow Brook at 3:25 p.m. Mother is in the lobby and is very agitated. I take her back to her room to look at her Easter basket. She wants to go to the bathroom. She is soaking wet, BM on her gown, robe, and restraint. She has not gone back to bed since she ate lunch. My bet is that no one has taken her to the bathroom or cleaned her since before lunch. How can human beings be so robbing of one's dignity?

I report this to the nurse. I also tell her that Mother has black diarrhea and has had for some time. This is the first the nurse seems to know of this. I talk with the Director of Nursing about weight-bearing on Mother's legs when CNAs are taking her to the bathroom. I am afraid she is going to get hurt transferring herself to the commode. Also, no change in medication has been made for her. The social worker, Kay, tells me that she will talk with the nurse practitioner tomorrow. How long are we going to let Mother suffer needlessly?

Tuesday, April 2, 1996

I arrive at Meadow Brook at 3:30 p.m. Mother is again very agitated. She has been all day, according to the CNA. Kay talked with the nurse practitioner. They are going to change her medication. She will finally be taken off Ativan and Haldol dosage will be increased, but the order has not been written. I will talk with her tomorrow.

I take her to the bathroom. She is soaked and has diarrhea. I put her in bed to change her. I talk to Kay again regarding transferring Mother in the bathroom—the weight-bearing issue—and the possibility of her getting hurt.

Wednesday, April 3, 1996

I arrive at Meadow Brook at 4:30 p.m. Mother is at the table in the dining hall with paper and pencil doing math figures, and she has fallen asleep. The nurse stops me in the hallway to tell me about the medication change. Ativan has been stopped! Haldol has been decreased to just the 10 a.m. dose, and they will start Klonopin three times daily. The nurse practitioner does not have time to talk with me. Kay has gone for the day. Some things I do not understand. When I left yesterday, I thought we had the medication straightened out—no Ativan, increase Haldol. Today all that has changed. What has happened?

Thursday, April 4, 1996

I arrive at 3:15 p.m. Mother is ballistic again! The nurse reports that she will not let anyone near her—not even to take her to the bathroom—and has been this way since lunchtime. She started Klonopin at 2 p.m. By 4 p.m., I was able to get her to agree to let me put her in bed to change her. She was soaked beyond imagination and has diarrhea, which I showed to the nurse. The nurse said she was not aware that Mother was having diarrhea. Does anyone in this place communicate with each other? I really think they need to pay me for her care.

I talk with Kay. I do not yet understand the medication change as ordered. Mother needs Haldol to keep her calm. It is the only medication to date which has worked for her. This is documented back to her hospital stay last August. Sitting in urine and BM all day is abuse of my mother by the medical personnel who refuse to give her the medication she needs to remain calm. I leave at 4:30 p.m. Mother is again ballistic!

I get to my car and completely lose it. Why, why, why is this happening to my mother? She is like a caged animal struggling to be free. She screams, "I am tormented" and no one listens except me. I scream, "She is tormented!" and no one will listen. Does anyone care? Where is there peace in any of this for Mother—for me? Why do we treat God's children in this manner?

The genteel Southern Lady now reduced to a caged animal. God help us all in this fight to save one of your children. I cry hysterically all the way to my church. I get out of my car. My minister, Allen is coming up the walkway. I go to him and fall apart saying, "If there were but one person on the face of this earth who could assume the care of my mother, I would blow my brains out!"

Allen takes me into his office. I sit down and tell him that this is now a hopeless situation for me.

I tell him that I am not really going to blow my brains out, but it is just how I feel at this point. I am blocked at every point from giving her the gift of peace for the remainder of her life by people who really do not care and by stupid laws, but I will go on trying out of the love I feel for her and for the gifts she has given me all my life. It is the least I can do for her. To cash it all in now would be to let her down, and this I will not do.

Allen hugs me and holds me, letting me feel his love and support, and tells me that he will do anything in his power to help me give Mother a gift of peace in her life. I go home.

At 7 p.m., the nurse calls me. Mother is still out of control. She has been fighting the nurse and has torn her arm open again. They want me to come back to Meadow Brook and see if I can calm her down. Do I look like a miracle worker?

I go back to Meadow Brook. I ask the nurse to call the doctor. Mother is worse than they said. She is swinging from every rafter ever made and does not appear to ever be coming down. I talk with the doctor by phone. He orders a shot of Ativan to be given to her immediately. It takes the nurse, myself, and four other CNAs to hold her down to give her the shot.

At 8:30 p.m., I am finally able to get Mother in bed. She is beyond soaked and has diarrhea. She has not been changed since this afternoon. I clean her, change her gown, and straighten her bed for her. I cry at her bedside. I promise her that if it is the last thing on earth that I do, I will make things better for her. I cannot change what has happened to her. Alzheimer's is cruel to everyone. But I can get medication for her that can give her a degree of peace, and I will—somehow, someway.

I sit with her and hold her hand until the shot takes effect and she falls asleep. I look at the peace on her face as she sleeps and vow to continue my fight.

Good Friday, April 5, 1996

I am up early and go to Meadow Brook. My thoughts are that on this Good Friday, I believe God and Jesus are shedding tears with me today. I just feel that they are as sad I am, and if they could change things for Mother, they would. I ask only for the strength to deal with anything regarding her today.

I plan to the have the doctor and/or nurse practitioner come to Meadow Brook today to see her. Something must be done. Mother is asleep when I arrive at 6:30 a.m. She has been given Klonopin. She is restless and awakens agitated. I clean her and get her up.

She remains agitated in the dining hall. I help her eat breakfast. Mother is not able to keep liquids in her mouth and is having difficulty swallowing. I call for the Director of Nursing, the Assistant Director of Nursing, the social worker, and the nurse on call. I show them what they have done to my mother. Kay is alarmed. She immediately puts in a call to the doctor.

Since this is a holiday weekend, we only get to talk with the doctor on call for the Clinic. We explain the situation. Finally at 9:15 a.m., orders are given for Haldol to be given to Mother three time daily. She is to have nothing else unless a shot of Ativan is needed in a crisis situation.

I put her back in bed at 9:40 a.m. She looks like death warmed over and needs rest. What in the hell is wrong with this world? Why would anyone treat another human being like Mother has been treated by the medical personnel? Do they just not care? Is she just another number and more money in their pocket? Or does it just not matter to anyone but me?

I will continue to monitor the Haldol dosage for the next several days to determine if it is enough. We have yet to knock her out except with Ativan for emergencies. I pray that very soon we will find the dosage which will give her peace. I will not give up trying—for other than my continued love day-to-day, it is the only gift I have left to give her. She deserves nothing less at this time. I wish there could be more

I wish her family could see and help her and me through this also. I pray to God that their eyes may be opened and their love will be put into action. Mother needs it. And selfishly, I pray that I may be included in that love. The silence is deafening on the home front as I walk this journey with Mother alone.

At this Easter, I pray not only for a resurrection of love from those who profess to love, but I also pray for the courage and wisdom to deal with what I cannot change. God grant me peace so that I may continue being a peacemaker in Mother's life.

As I am preparing to leave Meadow Brook, a young lady named Barbara stops me in the hallway. She works with a psychiatrist that did an evaluation of Mother back in November. She asks if there is anything she can do to help her. I tell her that I will let her know if there is. Right now we are fine. Mother does not need psychotherapy—she only needs the right amount of medication to give her some peace and that the Klonopin the psychiatrist suggested for her to take last November was prescribed for her two days ago and has ruined her. End of conversation.

Saturday, April 6, 1996

I arrive at Meadow Brook at 10:45 a.m. Mother is in the dining hall. She is calm. I do her hair and give her a manicure. I stay and have lunch with her. She is very sweet and remains calm throughout my visit. I put her back in bed after lunch. These small gifts of peaceful visits with Mother make my heart smile when they occur, and they do, indeed, bring joy to the journey. Kay reported to me that she was slightly agitated in the early morning but was okay by 10 a.m. I leave at 1:45 p.m.

Easter, Sunday, April 7, 1996

I arrive at Meadow Brook at 10:30 a.m. Mother is in the dining hall reading the paper. She is very calm. The church service is on TV. Today is a very emotional day for me. When the choir and congregation begin to sing "Christ The Lord Is Risen Today," I lose it and have to leave the room for a few minutes. I know that God is with me, and I feel Him very close on this day. I also realize that this is the last Easter that I will share with my mother. I eat lunch with her and our Meadow Brook friends.

A friend of mine, Barbara, walks up as we are finishing our meal. Barbara's mother died a year ago, and she could not stop thinking about my mother on this day. She visited with her a few minutes, and then we went out to her van and talked. It was so good to share some of my experience with someone who I knew had been there and could understand and love me through this day.

After lunch, Mother wants to go back to bed. I take her, change her, and put a fresh gown on her. John and his family come by for a few minutes. She falls asleep. I walk them out and break down, begging for help, and for their love.

I leave at 1:45 p.m. The notes in Mother's chart indicate that she is doing well with her new medication. The nurse reports some morning agitation. Maybe they need to adjust the times the medication is given to her to help carry her through the morning. I will ask tomorrow. Here we go again.

Monday, April 8, 1996

I arrive at Meadow Brook at 10:15 a.m. Mother is agitated. I roll her around all over the building. This seems to help. I talk with the nurse. Seems they have forgotten to give Mother her medication. I give it to her. She calms down after medication.

I stay and eat lunch with her. She only weighs 96 pounds. It is so hard to believe. I talk with Kay. We both agree that another dose of Haldol should be added to carry her through from 4 p.m. until 10 a.m. Hopefully, the nurse practitioner will agree to this. We have more than enough documentation to warrant it.

Tuesday, April 9, 1996

I arrive at Meadow Brook at 2 p.m. Mother is in the bathroom. The CNA has just sat her back down on the commode as she says she feels faint. I ask her to get the nurse. The nurse comes and helps me get Mother into her chair. She is extremely agitated.

She would not go to bed after lunch. She has not taken her 12:30 p.m. medication. I ask the nurse to give Mother her medication at 2:15 p.m. I ask why it could not be given by injection if she refuses to take it by mouth. She says that it could, but she was just waiting to see if she would take it by mouth. And how long, pray tell, are you going to wait? How agitated do we have to let her get? And, her next dose is at 4 p.m. Why can we not set a thirty-minute limit for her?

Mother has torn her arm open again from fighting. Why do they let her get to this point? I am still trying to check on an extra dose of Haldol. The bottom line is they need to give her the doses she is already supposed to take when she is supposed to take them. That only makes sense to me—but who am I?

Wednesday, April 10, 1996

I arrive at Meadow Brook at 9:30 a.m. Mother is in the dining hall. She needs to go to the bathroom. She is slightly agitated. I take her to the bathroom. She takes her 10 a.m. medication and looks at the paper. She is calm again.

I leave around 10:30 a.m. to run some errands. I return at 11:45 a.m. Mother is eating lunch and is very calm and sweet. Hopefully, with adding another dose of Haldol periodically, life can be better for her.

Friday, April 12, 1996

I talk with Kay. I tell her that I am giving up. I cannot fight this battle any longer. My quest to give my mother peace is no longer in my hands.

No matter what changes in medication are made, I now hold the doctor and Meadow Brook responsible for her safety. There is no reason for her to be hurt if she is properly medicated. I tell Kay that I am holding them responsible for abuse if Mother sits in urine and feces due to agitation and the staff not being able to change her.

I tell Kay that I will also hold them responsible if she no longer eats and drinks as a result of medication. It is now in their ball court for I do not seem to have the power to make it better for Mother. I just continually hate to see her suffer because of government regulations. How cruel can we be to human beings? I just cannot believe this is the world God intended it to be. We surely have mucked it up big time! Kay is going to talk with the doctor and the nurse practitioner and relay my feelings to them.

Saturday, April 13, 1996

I arrive at Meadow Brook at 10 a.m. Mother is in the dining hall looking at the paper. I give her a manicure. I leave at 11:20 a.m. She is in an excellent mood—laughing and smiling again! Today there is joy in our journey!

Sunday, April 14, 1996

I arrive at Meadow Brook at 10 a.m. Mother is in the dining hall looking at the paper. I stay and have lunch with her. I take her outside after lunch for a little while. She is in good humor.

She goes back to bed at 1 p.m. I talk with the nurse regarding medication. The nurse admits that Haldol really works for Mother and agrees that another dose would be good for her. She will talk with the nurse practitioner tomorrow. It has been a good week for Mother, given her circumstances. It will be such a shame to mess it all up once again with some silly medication change. I really feel hopeless and am just sorry that it is not in my power to control peace for her life as she walks her last days of her journey.

Monday, April 15, 1996

I arrive at Meadow Brook at 10:45 a.m. Mother is in the dining hall drinking a milkshake. I take her robe off. She is very hot. She is in a good mood.

After lunch, she takes a nap for an hour. I talk with the nurse practitioner. She is leaving Mother on Haldol three time daily—just changing the times to 6 a.m., 2 p.m., and 8 p.m. She is adding sleep medication to be given anywhere from 10 p.m. until 3 a.m. She is very nice to me and explains that she knows that I am right about Mother's medication. She just has to obey regulations. But, we will try this time change for a while and see if it continues to work.

She is also adding Carnation Instant Breakfast for Mother to see if she can halt her weight loss. I thank God for our meeting. I don't know what changed her mind about the medication change. I have a feeling it could be my comments about responsibility being shifted from me to them, but whatever, I am just grateful that something worked. Let's hope that this medication formula will work and continue to keep Mother in a good mood.

Tuesday, April 16, 1996

I arrive at 3:45 p.m. Mother is agitated. I roll her to her room. Everything is a mess due to wax being applied to floors. I straighten her room for her while she watches. She calms down slightly. We go back to the dining hall. I get her some orange juice.

The nurse gave her Haldol at 1 p.m. instead of 2 p.m. as Mother was very agitated. Why do they even have medication schedules in place? Guess tonight will be long for Mother. She has been to the beauty shop and has another skin tear on her arm. Here we go again.

Wednesday, April 17, 1996

I arrive at Meadow Brook at 3:30 p.m. Mother is in bed. She is very sweet and calm. We share lots of love together. This is another one of those Meadow Brook Moments, which I see as a gift that causes a light to burn brightly within my heart as I experience a moment in time filled with joy in the journey.

I leave at 4:20 p.m.

Thursday, April 18, 1996

I arrive at Meadow Brook at 3:40 p.m. Mother is in the dining hall—extremely agitated. I roll her around. She wants to go to the bathroom. We must wait for the CNA. Mother goes crazy—hitting, clawing, grabbing, etc. After going to the bathroom, she calms down.

I take her back to the dining hall and get her some orange juice. The nurse comes to change the bandage on her arm. I leave and return at 6:30 p.m.

Mother is still very agitated. I roll her around. I discover from her chart that her problem is she has not had her medication all day. What in God's name is going on? I am too tired to fight.

I go to the Family Council Meeting. I go back to Mother's room before I leave at 8:15 p.m. Mother is dozing but wakes up when I enter her room. She has finally had her medication. She is very sweet. I hug her, hold her, sit on her bed with her, share lots of love. My tears flow. I wish all her times could be this peaceful for her. She deserves nothing less. There just seems to be no way for this to happen. This has to be the most devastating disease for anyone to suffer through.

Friday, April 19, 1996

I arrive at Meadow Brook at 5:45 p.m. Mother is in the dining hall. She has thrown her pillow and lap robe off on the floor. A CNA is trying to force feed her. She continues to refuse to eat. I go to the nurse and ask how long she has been like this. She gets Mother's chart. Seems like all day.

I ask if she has had her medication on schedule. She checks the medication chart and tells me, "No." I ask if she still has the shot of Ativan given PRN. She says, "Yes," and asks me if I want her to give it to Mother. What am I? Her doctor?

I take Mother to her room as the TV is blaring and the CNA is continuing to force feed her. The nurse comes and gives her a shot of Ativan. I put her into bed.

I stay until 7:15 p.m. Mother finally is calm. Hopefully, the shot will help her sleep. Why do the nurses not know what times and what medication is available for Mother? I really should be on the payroll at Meadow Brook! Does it take an act of Congress to get this straightened out? It is time to end her suffering. Give her medication on time and supplement it with whatever it takes to give her peace. Is that too much to ask? Mother is a human being. Let's treat her like one and give her peace. Is that so hard? Must be. And this is a good nursing home?

Saturday, April 20, 1996

I arrive at Meadow Brook at 9:45 a.m. Mother is in the dining hall asleep. She wakes up at 10:00 a.m. She is slightly agitated. I roll her up to be weighed. She now weighs 95 pounds.

At 11:15 a.m., the nurse brings Mother's medication. She puts nine pills in front of her and asks me to give them to her. I asked why she did not have her medication on time. She says that it was because she was not in her room. Any excuse will do, won't it?

I ask her why she cannot give Mother her medication. She says that she does not have time. She leaves. I give Mother her medication. I seek out another nurse to find out what all those pills are. I discover that not only did she duplicate two of the pills, but also that the Haldol was three-and-a-half hours late being given. It just blows my mind that it does not seem to matter to anyone other than me whether Mother gets her medication on time, and no one is concerned that she just took too many pills. No one seems to know what they were. Here we go again.

Sunday, April 21, 1996

I arrive at Meadow Brook at 10:15 a.m. Mother is in her wheelchair at the bathroom sink with a

CNA taking a sponge bath. The CNA is telling her to stand up at the sink. I turn the corner into the bathroom and inform the CNA that Mother cannot bear weight on her legs. I show her the sign on the bathroom wall that says not to let her bear any weight on her legs. Perhaps there needs to be a reading course given? Glad I arrived when I did!

I put Mother back to bed after her bath. I eat lunch with her in her room. She is calm and in good humor. I give her a manicure after lunch. I leave at 1 p.m.

Tuesday, April 23, 1996

I arrive at Meadow Brook at 4 p.m. Mother is out of control. She has not had her medication. I go to her room and pick up her laundry. God help me! I hate this! I cannot take this anymore. I cannot bear to watch Mother go through this cruelty. I go home and cry.

Wednesday, April 24, 1996

I arrive at Meadow Brook at 3:30 p.m. Mother is in the dining hall. She is in a great mood.

A nurse comes to take blood from her arm. When he asks her to "Give me your arm," Mother looks at him and replies, "Why don't you just take it with you, do what you've got to do, and then bring it back?" He looks at her strangely. Mother laughs and says, "What? You can't take a joke?"

I don't think anyone knows how to take her at this moment. It has been so long since Mother told a joke. Another one of those special moments in time at Meadow Brook that I will always remember—a moment that brought joy to my life and to the lives of Mother's Meadow Brook friends!

I leave at 4:35 p.m.

Thursday, April 25, 1996

I arrive at Meadow Brook at 4 p.m. Mother is in an extremely good mood. She has had her medication on time for two days in a row now. Amazing! She wants to go to bed. I take her back to her room and put her in bed. We share a beautiful, peaceful time together before I leave.

Friday, April 26, 1996

Mother is slightly agitated when I arrive at Meadow Brook at 3:45 p.m. I take her with me to her room to put her clean gowns in her closet and to gather her laundry.

I take her back to the dining hall. I leave her with two other ladies reading the paper. I hug her. She

asks me how much I love her. I say, "A bushel and
a peck and a hug around the neck." Then I ask her,
"And what else?" Mother replies, "And a smile."

When I get to the door at the end of the hallway,
I look back. Mother is smiling and blows me a kiss
with her frail little hand. I thank God for moments
as special as this for it fills my heart with so much
goodness and joy, not just for me, but also for
Mother. For you see, deep inside her frail body and
jumbled mind, she is still there!

Sunday, May 12, 1996

It is Mother's Day. I arrive at Meadow Brook at
10 a.m. I take flowers for the tables in the dining
hall. I thought this would be a nice touch and a
special treat for everyone on this day—especially
for all those whose families do not come to see them
on this special day. I eat lunch with Mother.

Barbara, a friend of ours, comes by as we are
finishing lunch. She just wanted to come by and
share with Mother for a little while. Today is hard
for Barbara as her mom died this past year. I feel
so blessed to have been able to share a part of her
pain on this day.

John and his family come by. It is too much for
Mother. She is off her schedule and around 1:30

p.m. she loses it. I ask the family to leave and let me get her back in her bed. Mother cries to go home. I ask the nurse finally to give her a shot.

I leave reluctantly. It is hard to be the one to walk out on her when she is like this. My heart aches for her, and I long for her to be released. It is truly a long journey home, and I am worn out. Mother is, too. The rest of this day my heart is too full to be productive. But then there will always be tomorrow.

FROM THIS POINT ON, THE DAYS ARE PRETTY MUCH THE SAME. Mother has developed pneumonia and has lost the strength to fight. Some call pneumonia the 'Old Folks Friend,' and I think that they are right. My journal skips from Mother's Day to the last thirteen days of her life. Maybe nothing else in between matters. It just follows that such a special day would be followed by a time I call, "Peace in the Midst of the Storm." The storm has raged in our lives for so long. Today I see a break in the clouds. So, read on and understand why.

PEACE IN THE MIDST OF THE STORM

May 21 to June 11, 1996
May 21, 1996

*It is thirteen school days before the school year
will be over for me. I wonder how I have made it
through another one. I wonder how I have survived
the storm which has ravaged our lives this past year.
I wonder how much longer I can go on and how
much longer Mother will have to suffer as she has.*

*As I drive from my school to Meadow Brook, I
ponder this. I arrive at my somewhat usual time of 4
p.m. Mother is sitting in her wheelchair in her room
looking out the window. This is most unusual in and
of itself. Her back is to the door.*

*As I approach her, I greet her with my usual, "Hi,
Mother." She looks up into my eyes and replies,
"Hi, Honey. How was your day at school?" I am
taken aback by her immediately responding to me
as "Honey" and with the clarity of her mind to ask
how my day at school was.*

I reply, "It was rather hellacious, but it is over, and I am here with you now." She then asks me, "How many more day of school do you have left?" I respond, "Thirteen." She says, "That's good, Honey." I reply, "Yes, it is." I then question her as to why she feels that this is good. She looks into my eyes for what seems an eternity and responds, "Then I can go home to Mama and Daddy and your daddy." Tears fill my eyes as I respond, "Yes, you can."

To understand the irony of this conversation, you must remember that Mother and I had a standing joke with each other. Since every member of her family had died by age seventy-four of a heart attack, we were always sure she would follow suit. I would kid her and say, "If you are planning 'the Big One,' please do it in the summer. I do not have time for such during my school year." We would laugh together, and more than once, Mother would reply, "This I will do." And thus, thirteen days before summer vacation, Mother had scheduled her death.

We follow our usual routine, and I leave her in the dining hall with a hug and a smile. As I walk down the hallway to leave, I stop and turn around. Mother is still smiling and with her feeble hand reaches up and blows me a kiss.

As I push open the doors to leave Meadow Brook, I cry and say, "Yes, it is her smile and the moments of joy from this journey at Meadow Brook that I will always remember."

Today, the rest of the storm we have lived through just does not seem to matter. I know that the days are dwindling down to a precious few. A part of me cries in joy that her torment will be over. Another part of me cries knowing that to end this torment, I must lose my mother forever.

Driving home, I realize that I want to spend these precious days with Mother. To do that, I must take care of paperwork for school, arrange with my Principal to take time off, and develop a schedule that alternates me with home and Meadow Brook that will allow me to spend every moment I can with her until my leave is officially set.

I go home and take care of Mother's laundry. I sit down and open my briefcase and work until the wee hours of the morning on school paperwork. I get a couple of hours sleep before it is time to begin another day. I feel good knowing I have a plan.

May 22, 1996

I arrive later than usual at Meadow Brook due to a conference with my Principal to set up my leave. I have not set the exact date but assure him that all

*paperwork will be in order, and my children will be
taken care of in my absence. He is so understanding
and gives me the flexibility to set my date and just
let him know.*

*Mother is still in bed when I arrive, making her
usual attempts to get out. As I enter her room, I say
to myself, "Oh, please do not let her be agitated. I
am so tired and do not think I can deal with that. I
also have wonderful news to share with her. Please,
please, bring back reality to us today.*

*I greet her, and she asks to get up. I put her bed
rails down and sit on her bed saying, "Before you
get up, I have some very special news to share
with you." I begin, "Late yesterday afternoon, you
became a Great-Grandmother." Her face lights
up like a Christmas tree, and she replies, "Kelly
had her baby." I was so shocked, I almost fell off
the bed. Mother actually remembered Kelly was
pregnant and was having a baby!*

*She asks all the right questions. "Did Kelly have
a boy or a girl? What is his name? How much does
he weigh? How long is he?" And then she says, "I
must get up and go see her in the hospital."*

*My heart sinks knowing that this is not possible.
I talk with her, explaining how far away the hospital
is and that we cannot go today. Mother seems to
accept this and says, "Well, we will just wait until*

*Kelly and David get home from the hospital to go
and see them." I reply, "Yes, Mother, that would be
a good idea." I then offer to take her down to the
phone and let her call Kelly.*

*We complete our afternoon routine: Changing her
diaper, putting on a fresh gown, putting on a fresh
robe, and getting her into her wheelchair. Mother is
so excited. She says, "Can I really talk with Kelly?"
I say, "Of course, you can, Mother." I take her to
the phone, and she has a beautiful conversation with
Kelly. She tells Kelly how proud she is of her and
how proud she is to be a Great-Grandmother. As
I listen, I cannot believe the sensible conversation
Mother is having with Kelly. Other than asking over
and over, "What did you name your baby?" the
conversation is reality-based.*

*I take off my glasses as the tears fall softly. The
look on Mother's face is one that I have seen many
times in my life. It is the look of overwhelming
gratitude to God for the wonder of life. Love is
written in every line of her beautiful face. And for
another moment in time, she is back with us. Another
brief Meadow Brook moment of joy in the journey.*

*After the phone conversation, I take Mother to
the dining hall to get her afternoon orange juice.
She asks me to get the paper for her. She then
reaches up, runs her fingers through my hair, and*

says, "Honey, I love you. Thank you for letting me talk with Kelly. I know that you must get to class. You go on, and I will be fine." We hug with bushels and pecks and a smile.

Today, as I get to the end of the hallway to leave, I turn and blow her a kiss. She returns it. In my car, the tears once again flow. Yesterday marked the beginning of the end, but today marks the return of my mother (who as it turned out would be with us all of her remaining days). I thank God for the gift of His joyous miracles in our lives.

I returned to Meadow Brook in the evening. Mother was in her bed sleeping. I did not wake her—just sat beside the bed looking at her and remembering all the wonder-filled moments in our lives. She looks so peaceful sleeping this evening. I do not stay long. As I am leaving her room, I turn around to look at her. I feel a peace that I cannot explain. It is a peace "that passeth all understanding," but it is enough to comfort my frail heart and allow me to leave Mother to go home and get some rest.

May 23, 1996

I arrive at Meadow Brook at 3 p.m. Mother is up and sitting in her room again. After greeting her, we go down to look at the aviary. How she loves to watch the little finches. She is fascinated with their movement. Last Sunday as we watched them, she named them. Today she calls them by name— Goldie, Scarlett, Frick, and Frack. Her eyes track their every movement, and she comments from time to time on their activity.

After thirty minutes, I take her to the dining hall and get her some juice. She asks for some of the new magazines I have brought to her. I go back to her room to get them. Something makes me look on her nightstand. I see a couple of small pieces of paper that she has written on. The first sentence begins: "Oh, Nancy, there are not enough words to tell you how much I love you. I thank you for all the loving care you have given me throughout my life— especially in this place. I want you to know that I never meant to lose you . . . and, I really didn't. I only lost your name. So, forgive me, please."

I sat on her bed and let the tears fall. I left the note on the nightstand. Guess I was hoping she would add more to it, but when it was still there the next afternoon, I took it home with me.

I took her several magazines. She enjoyed looking at them and talking with me about the pictures. She talks with the CNAs that were going off duty and speaks to the ones coming on duty. After a while, she looks at me and says, "You can go now. I know that you have so much to do and I will be fine."

I go and gather her laundry, come back for my special hug, and leave for the day. It has been an exceptionally good time of sharing with Mother!

Once again, I go back to Meadow Brook in the evening. Mother is sleeping peacefully, and I sit with her for a while. I thank God for another beautiful day in our lives and for His sustaining goodness throughout our journey. I leave Meadow Brook in peace.

May 23 to May 30, 1996

This next week of Mother's life, she has been herself. I have enjoyed my afternoon visits and have even looked forward to them. She is calm most of the time. She is weaker with each visit as she now has pneumonia and some afternoons is still in bed. These are the miracle times that I have wished to share with her. These are the peaceful times. I have tried so hard to give her these times every day, but until now, it has been to no avail. Now she is giving them to me. I accept this gift into my heart with gratitude to God for His miracle in our lives.

On Saturday, my good friend, Lynn, came to Charlotte to go to Meadow Brook with me. I will always remember that day. We were both amazed

that Mother knew her, called her by name, asked about her girls, and had a very memorable time of sharing with both of us. We talked about teaching with Mother. I was able to get her to recite some of her childhood poems for Lynn. How I wished I had brought my camcorder with me to record this moment of joy in our lives!

Mother smiled and laughed and brought love to our lives. And yet, each day as I leave her to go home, I have the sinking feeling that it might be her last. Each goodbye brings me to tears. Even having suffered through the storm with her, it is not easy to give her up. I cry most of the way home each day and still return to Meadow Brook each evening to sit and watch her sleep peacefully. Life is good at the present. I know it is not going to last. My heart breaks. I wish there were someone to share all of this with on a daily basis.

May 31, 1996

I am at school and around 9:20 a.m., a call comes for me from Meadow Brook. It is the nurse telling me that Mother is extremely lethargic and not doing well. Her vital signs have been fluctuating during the night. I ask the nurse to transfer me to Kay's office. I explain what the nurse has told me to Kay.

I ask her to do down and assess the situation and call me back at school.

About thirty minutes later, Kay returns my call. She tells me that with pneumonia and the fluctuation of vital signs it does not look good. I ask her if I should come immediately. She replies, "I cannot tell you not to come." That was good enough for me.

I quickly place a call to John at the church. He is at the hospital with people whose family member is having surgery. The secretary pages him there, and he calls me at school. I explain the circumstances to him, emphasizing that it could be a matter of days, a matter of hours, or a matter of minutes for Mother. He says that he will try to get by Meadow Brook in the afternoon. I blow a fuse. "What do you mean in the afternoon? Did you hear what I said to you? It could be minutes." He replies, "What good could I do if I were there? I have been there once already this week." I replied, "You could hold your mother's hand and tell her that you love her. He said before I could slam the receiver down, "I have already done that once this week." I am in a rage.

I proceed to talk with Principal and get his permission to begin my leave. I call my deacon, Chet, and let him know the circumstances. I go back to my classroom, talk with my co-workers,

letting them know where all of my paperwork is so they can turn it in for me. I thank them for being so understanding about my not coming back to finish the school year. They are so kind and simply say, "Go. We will be okay."

I arrive at Meadow Brook around 10:30 a.m. When I enter Mother's room, John and Chet are there. Mother is semi-comatose at this point. There is no response from her. She continues like this all day. It is at this point that I make Meadow Brook my home, too. Mother does not have a roommate, and I simply push the other bed next to hers. I call it our "double wide—side by side." I know I will not leave her again except to go home once a day to shower, do her laundry, and look after the cats.

I experience my first night of trying to sleep in a nursing home. The noises are unbelievable. I sleep fitfully, listening mostly to Mother's breathing. At 2:30 a.m., her eyes come open. She looks at me beside her and says, "Well, good morning, Nancy." I reply, "Good morning, Mother." She says to me, "I need to wake up and ask you a question. May I give my life to God?" I reply, holding her close, "You certainly may, but you know, Mother, you did that a long time ago. Why would you ask that now?" She replies, "My long journey is over, and I want to go home."

I look into her sad worn-out eyes and give her

permission to go. (That was the first of many times to come that I would assure her that it was okay to go home. It never got easier.) We hug and hold each other into the morning.

Mother does not speak again until Saturday morning. I do not sleep. I keep looking at her, realizing how much I will miss her—her wisdom, her love, her smile, her hand holding mine no matter what, her laugh, her faith, the force of good that she has been in my life. I startle myself as I realize that all of those things will be with me forever for they are in my heart. I have to laugh that there is a part of me that will even miss Meadow Brook.

Saturday, June 1, 1996

Mother is still sleeping. I go and have a cup of coffee. When I return, she is still asleep. I sit and watch her sleep as I hold her hand. She has fought the good fight and is now finishing her course. I give her back to God with gratitude, which no man can measure. She will always be a part of my life, and I know that someday I will be with her again. The hour she will go is in God's hands. I will wait with her so that her passage is eased by the love felt here and the love greeting her on the other side.

Mother awakens momentarily, looks at me and says, "Honey, I will miss you." I hug her and say, "I will miss you too, Mother. But it is okay. I will be okay." My beautiful angel seems ready to take flight. "Mother, it is my wish that you go in peace and with my love. Know that you will live on in my heart forever."

Mother continues to drift in and out of sleep. I take this time to write her obituary. I know that even though this is one of the hardest things I have ever done, it is easier doing it while she is living than after she is gone.

Mother awakens and wants to get up and have breakfast. I bathe her, put a fresh gown and robe, and take her to the dining hall. As she waits for her breakfast, she looks around, looks at me, and asks, "How did we ever get mixed up with all of these old people?" I had no reply other than, "I don't know, Mother." The explanation would simply take too long! But this is one of the times I will never forget.

After eating a little breakfast, she wants to go back to bed. Around 10 a.m., our good friend, Martha, comes to visit. Mother awakens again and knows who she is. John comes a little later. I take this opportunity to go home to shower, change clothes, do Mother's laundry, and take care of the cats.

When I return, I find Mother, Martha, and John sitting on the patio. What a shock. We all stay there for a few minutes. Mother sits and gazes at the clouds silently. Then she says, "I would like to be a cloud so I could fly away from this body and mind that has imprisoned me." I look into her eyes and see the weariness of the past few years, and I reply, "You would make a beautiful cloud, Mother."

In a few more minutes, we return Mother to her room and to her bed. Martha says her goodbyes to her. John stays a little while longer and then leaves. About thirty minutes later, Mother awakens and asks me to put her bed rails down. At this point, I have also removed her restraint and asked the nurses not to put it back on her. She is simply too weak to get up. I put the rails down.

Mother says, "Honey, sit here. I want to hold you." I sit on her bed, and we hold each other. She asks, "I'm not going to get well am I?" "No, Mother. I don't think you are. I think you are ready to go home. I think your journey is coming to a close. You will be going home to your mother and daddy, my daddy, your family, and to a host of other friends who have loved you dearly. "But, Honey," Mother says, "I will miss you terribly." "I will miss you too, Mother, but it is okay for you to go."

I lay her back down on her bed, and she goes back to sleep. John returns later in the afternoon. He and Mother sing hymns—"Amazing Grace" and "How Great Thou Art." Mother sings every word and keeps saying, "Sing it again."

She wants to get up. I get her into her wheelchair. She wants to go outside. At this point, she is exhibiting bizarre, repetitive behavior. John rolls her out for what I will call a walk on the wild side. He takes Mother up Parkway Drive and back again—over and over. She keeps saying, "Do it again."

We finally bring her back in, and I put her back to bed. She begins repetitive movements—hands on bed rails and raising herself up and down—repeating the last thing said to her over and over. Try as I might, I cannot break this chain of behavior. It is so bizarre, I have to get away.

John says that he can stay until 5 p.m. I stop on my way out and talk to the second shift nurse. I explain Mother's behavior to them and ask them to give her something to calm her down. I explain that this is not her typical agitated behavior. They assure me they will check on her and give her something.

I leave and go home to do more of her laundry and some of my own. I return to Meadow Brook at 6 p.m. She is in bed, lying in a pool of diarrhea with no diaper on. BM is all over the bed and her gown. I go and get a diaper and washcloths and towels. On the way down the hall, I stop the nurse and blow up, saying "I do not ever want to find my mother like this again."

Two CNAs were sent to Mother's room to clean her and to calm me down. I go and find the two second-shift nurses as Mother is still exhibiting her bizarre behavior from this afternoon. I ask them to check on her and to give her something to calm her down.

At 8:45 p.m., one of the nurses comes and gives Mother a Loritab. At 8:55 p.m., she begins shaking uncontrollably—tremors in her arms, legs, her whole body. I ring the call bell for help. A CNA comes, and I ask her to get a nurse STAT.

Five minutes later, a nurse appears. I ask her if she can explain what is going on with Mother. She says that the tremors are from the Haldol. I tell her that this is just not so. These are not Haldol tremors. I ask her to call the doctor. She said she would if I wanted her to, but he would only tell me the same thing. Therefore, we would be wasting his time. I asked her to get the other nurse. She says she will ask him to come to Mother's room when he gets off break. I ask how long that might be. She says, "Oh, thirty minutes or so." I go ballistic! "Not to be rude, but Mother is having seizure activity of some form, and if she goes into cardiac arrest and dies, what will you tell the doctor and the Administrator of this facility on Monday?"

A CNA comes to Mother's room. I ask her to stay with Mother and hold her arms gently so she would not hurt them flailing them against the bed rails. I run to call my minister, Allen. He comes within five minutes. The horror on his face when he walks into the room says it all. He comes over and relieves me.

Mother is thrashing about like a mad animal. Her eyes are wide open, staring at me as if to say, "Please make this stop." The fear on her face will forever be a part of my memory. She is not responsive. The other nurse finally arrives. He says that Mother did the same thing the other day when I had gone home. I asked him as nicely as possible why I had not been informed of this. He said that he did not want to upset me. Mother had an intestinal impaction. He cleaned her out and gave her Milk of Magnesia and hot coffee to drink.

After the nurse leaves, no one comes back to check on her until 11:30 p.m. I rest next to her, holding her hand. I get up and walk the halls. I drink coffee and sit outside in the cool night air for a while. What a nightmare this day has been. What if I had not been here? I will check her chart tomorrow and certainly will inform the Administrator and Director of Nursing about these incidents on Monday. For now, I only have the strength to hold her hand.

I stay at Meadow Brook through the weekend. Mother wakes up occasionally. She looks into my eyes with a weariness of heart and soul. She constantly says that she hurts when she is awake. I lay beside her in our created 'double wide', hold her hand, comfort her as much as I can. She drifts in and out of consciousness throughout the day Sunday.

I leave her at 7:30 p.m. on Sunday evening to go home to shower, do her laundry, check on the cats, and just get some fresh air.

I go back to Meadow Brook at 10 p.m. I curl up in the bed beside her. She is sleeping peacefully at this point. Throughout the night, she awakes occasionally. She squeezes my hand as she looks into my eyes. Her only words throughout the night are, "Nancy, I hurt."

Monday, June 3, 1996

I have slept fitfully through the night with Mother. My thoughts center on one thing—to not let Mother suffer with pain.

I ask for a meeting with the Director, Kay, and the Director of Nursing. We meet in the Director's office at 9 a.m. I tell them the events of the weekend and request that Mother's doctor be called, and I be given a chance to speak with him. I want to request a morphine patch be used with her to ensure that

she will not be in pain.

The Director asks me if I am aware of what that will mean. I tell him I know putting the patch on Mother will hasten her death. I have seen this so many times with friends dying from cancer. The Director of Nursing does not want me to do this. She wants to send Mother to the hospital for a CAT Scan to determine the cause of seizures she has experienced. Really? Just last night, you said all her shakes were from the Haldol she was taking! Won't fall for that one! I just look at her and explain to her that Mother is dying, and my only wish is that she not die in pain.

The Director calls the doctor, and I talk with him. The morphine patch will be ordered today. The only request that I have is that I be with Mother when it is applied.

I leave his office and go outside to the patio for a while. Decisions of this magnitude are tough even when you know it is what your loved one would want for themselves if they could speak for themselves. I ask God for the strength to complete Mother's long journey home with her—giving both of us the peace that passeth all understanding.

I go back in and spend the day loving Mother. She drifts in and out of consciousness throughout the day. I lay beside her. I walk the halls. I go outside occasionally. And I wait for the morphine patch to be delivered.

It is 5 p.m. before the patch is brought to her room. I look at the nurse and ask her to not put it on her until the morning. I need to go home to do Mother's laundry, take a shower, and get some rest. The nurse grants my request.

Mother awakens for a brief period after the nurse leaves. I explain to her that I am going home for a little while, and I will be back as soon as I can. She squeezes my hand as if to give her "Okay." I hug her and leave with tears streaming down my face.

I arrive home. I do the laundry. I take care of the cats. My thoughts are all-consuming at this point. I lay down on the sofa to just rest for a few minutes. I awaken at 5 a.m. I am in a panic. I cannot believe that I did this! I check the answering machine to see if there was a call from Meadow Brook. There was not! I get in the car and drive as fast as I can back to Meadow Brook.

Tuesday, June 4, 1996

I arrive back at Meadow Brook at 5:45 a.m. Mother is sleeping and continues to do so through the morning. The nurse brings the morphine patch at 9 a.m. When she leaves the room after putting on the patch, I cry. I hold Mother's hand and tell her that I have given her my gift of peace.

Around 1 p.m., Mother wakes up and says, "Hi, Nancy. I am back and want to talk with you about dying." I am taken aback by this but proceed to tell her that her dying would mean going home to her mother and daddy, and to my daddy. She looks up with a smile on her face and says, "Oh, Honey, do you know what a glorious day that will be?" I reply, "Yes, Mother and I want you to go. You have fought so hard for so long, and it is time that you have peace."

We simply hold each other for a long time. Mother looks into my eyes and says, "I have something I want you to do for me. I want you to write my eulogy, and I want you to speak at my Celebration of Life service. You are the only one who can tell people about my journey. Can you please do this one last thing for me?"

I cannot hold back the tears at this point. I promise Mother I will do this for her. She looks at me for several minutes and then says, "Honey, that would be the highest honor you could ever give me. You know, I want my service to be one of dignity and celebration. We have talked about it. You will know what to do."

Following this conversation, Mother goes back to sleep. While she is sleeping, I look around her room— this room that has been her home these last ten months. I listen to the sounds she has listened to day and night for the last ten months. I watch the people pass her doorway going up and down the halls as she has watched them for the past ten months. As difficult as it has been, I am able to see the good today. As horrid as it has been, Mother has been surrounded by people who love her. Maybe they did not always do things as I would have wanted them done—or as I felt Mother deserved to have them done—but, bottom line, they have loved my mother! And in my heart, I know they have loved me, too. In this love, I experience joy in this journey at Meadow Brook.

In the afternoon, Sue comes to visit. She has a great conversation with Mother about her life and John and me. During the conversation, Sue asks Mother how old she thinks I am. Mother looks up and smiles and says, "She is ancient." Sue asks Mother how old ancient is. Mother replies, "Oh, thirty-five or so." Mother's smile tells us that she has not lost her sense of humor even at this point.

Wednesday, June 5, 1996

I spend the night beside Mother. She stopped taking liquids last evening. She opens her eyes for brief periods of time throughout the night but with a blank stare. I work on writing her eulogy through the night.

While cleaning out things at home a couple of months ago, I came across the eulogy for the lady who was instrumental in finding me for Mother and Daddy to adopt. I kept it and now feel like there is a part of it that can be incorporated into Mother's eulogy. Guess I see it as a completion of a full circle of life for Mother, Daddy, and me. And, so I write. And, so I cry.

I doze for brief periods of time and write more. By morning, I have completed the eulogy. Mother opened her eyes around 10 a.m. and squeezed my hand. I take this golden opportunity to tearfully read her eulogy to her. She does not say anything but has the sweetest smile on her face.

I sit on her bed and hold her hands. I talk with her about her life and what it has meant to me. I pray with her, giving thanks to God for her life and all we have shared during the years. I cannot stop touching her baby-soft skin, hugging her frail body, running my fingers through her silver hair. I do not want to ever forget what she feels like.

Mother's hands were always the best. These hands have held me, fed me, changed me, spanked me when I needed it, comforted me, and have given me a love beyond compare.

Allen, our minister, comes by for a visit. He holds Mother's hands, looks at me, and says, "I wonder how many hands these hands have comforted in their lifetime?" I do not know the answer to that question except to say that the number could be totaled only by knowing the number of hands that needed Mother to hold them. For where there was a need, you could always find her holding a hand.

The CNAs are concerned that Mother is not eating or drinking. I ask the nurse to write an order, "Nothing by mouth." If Mother has chosen to stop eating and drinking, then I will honor that for her.

The next two days are much the same. I stay around the clock with her. Many times I sing to her. Oh, I cannot carry a tune in a bucket, but she loves to sing. I play tapes of old hymns that she loves. I just sit and hold her hand most of the time. Periodically, she squeezes my hand, letting me know that she knows I am there.

The minutes, hours, and days are long, but, I do not want Mother to die alone. I want to be with her. I just hope that I can physically continue keeping the hours needed to fulfill that wish. I want to be here holding her hand when her spirit takes flight.

God, I pray, give me the strength to continue.

The CNAs come one by one to Mother's room on Friday. The word has gone out that she is terminal. Each one who comes sits and holds her hand and tells her that they love her. They hug me and tell me they love me.

One special CNA sits with us in the afternoon before her shift is over. She says as she holds Mother's hand, "I will miss my buddy." Tears begin to flow down her cheeks. I hand her a Kleenex. I say, "I know. I will miss her, too. Do you know what I will miss most? I will miss her cursing. (And I thought I never would say that!) I guess I would love to see that feisty body rise up one more time."

"Yes," the CNA replies, "So would I. Your mother is a beautiful lady, and I will always remember her in my heart." I get up and go around the bed to hug her. That is the last time she saw Mother as she had the next four days off.

During this day, everyone from the Administration Staff to the Housekeeping Staff—anyone who had known Mother during her stay at Meadow Brook— come to hold her hand and say their goodbyes.

I remember sitting in the dining hall eating lunch with Mother one of the first months she was living at Meadow Brook. While eating, they rolled a body out in a body bag. I learned later that this was never supposed to happen, but it did. I remember thinking that one day that would be my mother.

For most people, nursing homes are a place people go to die. Maybe they have been forgotten by most of the world as we knew it to be. But, I know in my heart that these people at Meadow Brook have loved us and go on loving us each hour of each day. Ironic that this hell on Earth could resemble heaven. People who love have a way of giving that to us as their gift— freely given, no strings attached—just love.

Saturday continues much the same. Martha, Sue, and Chet come by to check on Mother and me. John comes in and out during the day. Mother seems fairly stable this evening, and I decide to go home to do laundry, shower, and get a couple of hours rest. I hold Mother's hand and tell her that I am leaving for a short while. "Hang in there, Mother. I will be back. You just need to wait." I leave.

Sunday, June 9, 1996

I awaken at 4:45 a.m. on the sofa in the den. I look at the clock, startled again that I could have done this. I check the answering machine and no calls have come in. I drive back to Meadow Brook.

It is 5:30 a.m. Mother is having difficulty breathing. I make the decision to put her on oxygen as a comfort measure.

I sit with her for the next few hours just holding her hand. I release her hand to stand up and perhaps take a walk, but her hand comes up in the air, reaching for me, and I sit back down and hold her hand again.

I make the decision to call John. I call his church and leave a message with a gentleman to let John know after his service that I need him to come to Meadow Brook. John is delivering the sermon at his church this morning, and I do not want him to get this message before the service.

I sit with Mother until John, Carolyn, and Josh arrive. We all cry together as we realize that the end is near. John has talked with Will and Kelly during the week, but they did not want to come and see their grandmother like this.

Carolyn asks me if I feel like she should call them now. I reply, "Yes. Tell them that their grandmother probably cannot see them, but that she can still hear them. Tell them what it would mean to her for them to hold her hand, and tell her that they love her. But make it their decision, and I will understand if they cannot do this."

Within twenty minutes Will and Kelly come. Will walks over to his grandmother, holds her hand and says, "Grandmother, it is Will. I just want you to know how much I love you." The tears are streaming down his young face. I tell him it is okay to cry. I hand him a Kleenex. Kelly is sitting on the bed holding her grandmother's hand. She, too, is crying. She cannot speak, but her tears tell of her love for her grandmother. I hand her a Kleenex.

All of a sudden, we notice tears falling softly down Mother's cheeks. We know at this point that she knows we are all here. I softly wipe her tears from her face, and then I wipe my own.

Everyone leaves with the exception of Will. He decides to stay with his grandmother and me for a while. Later in the afternoon Sue, Chet, and Allen come by. We do not see how Mother can make it through the night. Her heart is pounding, and we can hear the fluid in her lungs around her heart. There are many times when her breathing stops and then begins again.

Will and I each hold Mother's hands and talk with her and with each other. Sue comes back in the late afternoon. We decide to order pizza for dinner, and we all eat together in Mother's room.

At 11:30 p.m., I make Will leave. He has to go to work tomorrow and needs to go home and get some rest.

I stay with Mother. I want to hold her hand and let her know she is not alone. The nurse on duty makes me pots of coffee through the night, as I cannot sleep. At 4 a.m., Mother's vital signs stabilize, and I go home for a couple of hours to shower, do her laundry, and take care of the cats. I just need to get outside and get some fresh air and be away from the smell of death. Sometimes we just have all we can take and have to cling to the hope that life will hold on until we return.

Monday, June 10, 1996

I arrive back at Meadow Brook at 6:30 a.m. Mother is still having a struggle. We know she is not in pain as we have changed the morphine patch twice this week, but to see her little chest heave with each breath is sometimes unbearable.

I take her little tape player back this morning and play inspirational tapes. Around 9:30 a.m., Allen comes to visit. He is just as shocked as I am that Mother is still clinging to life. He is leaving Friday for a month. We decide that it is a good idea for him to tell her this. Allen takes Mother's hand and explains to her that if we cannot have her service Thursday and her burial on Friday morning, he will not be able to fulfill his promise to her to do both services for her.

I also tell her that tomorrow is my last day of school. Anyone listening to our conversation with Mother would say we are both crazy, but we need to let her know, and I believe that she does still hear us.

Allen and I are so afraid that he will not be here to officiate at Mother's Celebration Of Life and graveside service. I do not know if she can let go for us. Only God has the answer to this, but we talk to her anyway.

Chet comes by and also is astonished that Mother is hanging on. John comes and sits with us for a couple of hours. Sue comes and brings a picnic lunch for me. We sit on the front steps of Meadow Brook sharing it, complete with ants! The food tastes so good to me. I have not been eating much. Emotion and exhaustion have a way of taking away an appetite. I do know that people who love you make a difference in your life, particularly under these circumstances.

During the afternoon, the CNA comes by to change Mother's diaper. I am standing at the foot of the bed. When they pull her gown up, I have to leave the room. Neither eating nor drinking anything has reduced her little body to nothingness. How can she still be alive? Why is she still alive? One cannot describe the horror death sometimes brings, and it is probably best not to continue these thoughts.

Around 7 p.m., I have to leave. I am ready to fall on my face. John has come back and plans to stay until 9 p.m. Today is Jim's birthday. I pray Mother will hang on until tomorrow. I do not want her to die on his birthday. I ask John to call me before he leaves if there is any change, no matter what the hour.

This is my hardest goodbye. I tell Mother that I have to leave for a while, but that I really want her to be there when I return. She squeezes my hand,

and I know she has heard me. I have no guarantee that she will last. I am so torn as to leave or not, but I will be no good to anyone if I collapse. I leave after holding her hand for what seems like forever, in case I never have this opportunity again.

I go home and do Mother's laundry. I take care of the cats. I lay down on the sofa but cannot sleep. My mind keeps reliving these last months. My mind keeps reliving these last days. After a couple of hours, I get up and take a shower and drive back to Meadow Brook.

John has gone, and Mother and I are by ourselves in the quiet of her room. I take her hand to let her know I am back. She opens her eyes and says, "Oh, there you are. I knew you said you were coming back. I just did not realize you were here, Is tomorrow your last day of school?" she asks. I have tears streaming down my face at this point and simply say, "Yes, Mother, it is." She asks me if I still have her music with me? I tell her I do. She asks me to find and play "Softly and Tenderly" for her. As the song plays, her eyes close once more.

Mother continues her struggle to stay alive. Her breathing continues to be labored. I sit by her bed and hold her hand. I lay down beside her in our 'double wide' and hold her hand.

I get up for brief periods and get coffee and some fresh air outside. I cannot sleep.

At 4 a.m., Mother opens her eyes once again. She looks into my eyes and begins to cry. I let her. In a few minutes, I wipe her tears and simply say, "It is okay. Your journey is complete, Mother, and you can go home. I am so grateful to God for His gift of you to me. I am so grateful to God for letting us share our lives together for so many years. I love you so much. I will miss you always, but I know that you must go, and I want you to know that because of all the great life lessons you taught me, I will be okay." She smiles her sweet smile and simply says, "I love you, Nancy." At the time I did not know that those would be her last words.

John comes back to Meadow Brook around 9 a.m. Chet comes by. Allen comes back. He and John talk about Mother's Celebration Of Life service. Sue comes. Martha comes. And, so our day goes.

Around 10 a.m., I feel Mother's feet, and they are so cold. I remember being at my daddy's bedside as he was dying and experiencing the same feeling. I talk to John about what is happening. Mother continues her struggle to breathe. Periodically, she squeezes my hand, and I simply say, "I am here, Mother."

In the early afternoon, she is cold to her knees, and her hands have turned cold. Yet, she continues to breathe. Her eyes come open and do not close again—John on one side and me on the other, holding her hands and stroking her brow. I know that she is aware that we are both with her. Anytime I move my hand, her hand instantly comes up to find mine. Where her strength comes from at this point to even raise her hand is beyond my comprehension.

As the afternoon continues on, the nurse wants to know if I want them to increase Mother's oxygen. I tell them, "No." I tell them Mother is ending her journey and deserves the right not to prolong it. Many times throughout the afternoon, her eyes roll back, and she stops breathing for a second or two. Then miraculously she comes back to us.

At 6:55 p.m., John leaves to take a walk. We have alternated breaks throughout the day. I sit on Mother's bed—put my cheek to hers and tell her that is okay for her to go. I tell her that I love her enough to let her end her journey and go home. "It is time, Mother."

At 7:05 p.m., John returns from his walk. I ask him if he has given Mother permission to go. He says he has not. I ask him to do this, and I leave for a minute to give him his own time with her.

At 7:15 p.m., with John and me at her bedside holding her hands, Mother's chest heaves, her eyes roll back as if startled, she smiles, and she closes her eyes. I know that she is gone. I look at John and say, "Mother is gone, John" He replies, "But she still has a pulse." I tell him that it will stop momentarily. And it does.

I look out the window of her room at the huge oak tree in all of its beauty and say, "Thank you, God." Mother is at peace. She has gone home. She has completed her long journey home. John and I sit and hold her hands, crying. My tears are tears of joy for Mother's peace, but they are also tears for the emptiness I already feel. I get up and go to John. I hug him, and we both cry more. I suggest that we sit quietly with Mother for a few minutes. I do not want to leave her, but know I must. I guess no one wants to give up those they love and to cling to their earthly body for as long as possible.

The body is such a symbol of life, and even when the soul is gone, it gives us the strength to hold on. After about fifteen minutes, I go to tell Kay that Mother has died. The nurses come to clean her up. John asks me to call Carolyn. He cannot make the call. We then moved Mother's belongings to my car. I have already taken out all but one carload. After everything is gone, we go back in to say our goodbyes.

Mother looks so peaceful. The bed has been raised, and a fresh sheet is on top of her. I hold her hand one last time, rub those bruised arms which have held me and loved me all of my life. I already know that I will miss her touch forever. I kiss her cheek and let my tears fall softly on her beautiful face. My beautiful angel has taken flight. John and I leave around 8:30 p.m.

When I get home, Allen and Martha are sitting on the back deck. We unpack my car and move all of Mother's things into the guest room. Sue and Chet come over. We sit on the deck until after 10 p.m. I then collapse into bed. I feel at peace knowing Mother's suffering is over.

I know the real struggle of my finding peace will come in the days, months, and perhaps years to come as I attempt to come to terms with Alzheimer's and this terrible loss. Perhaps I should write a book? For now, I am exhausted mentally and physically from the long journey of the past few years. All I can do is give in to that exhaustion. My eyes close shortly after midnight.

The struggle for breath for Mother during her last few days is foremost in my mind, but I know that even in the end, she lived life abundantly—surrounded by love, she gave love until her last breath—and her love would always be in my heart and help to sustain me throughout my own journey.

I THINK ABOUT THE LAST DAYS OF OUR LIVES TOGETHER and thank God for the miracle He gave to us by giving me the gift of my mother back in my life. Before this happened, if someone had asked me if I believed in miracles, I probably would have said "No," or, "I really don't know."

After experiencing those last thirteen days with Mother—whose mind was restored in part from the devastation of Alzheimer's that destroyed her memory for years—I can say with certainty I do believe in miracles. As I begin to drift hopefully into a night of restful sleep, I know deep in my heart that it is Mother's gentleness, the touch of her hands, and her smile that I will always remember when I think back on these days. It is the moments of joy found in the midst of this journey that will always hold a sacred place in my heart. A place I can "go to" often to experience the joy found there.

AFTER THE RAIN

June 12 to June 14, 1996

On the outer edges of the storm that has hurled about us for these few years, there is now but a drizzle of rain that falls softly into all the lives that Mother has touched throughout her long journey home. For the next few days, that drizzle will sustain those who loved her most and bring peace to their lives through love shared by so many. These days are have-to days with responsibilities given to finishing the journey here on earth for Mother. There is much to be done and final plans laid into place as we begin to celebrate the life she lived among us.

June 12, 1996, to June 14, 1996
Wednesday, June 12, 1996

I awaken early. I feel like a zombie, but there is much to do on this day, so I force myself to get up. It is an effort to put one foot in front of the other, but I get up and take a shower. I sit in the den not really knowing what to do at this point.

Martha knocks at the door. She comes in and makes a pot of coffee. She is prepared to spend the day and coordinate the activities needed.

While I am sitting on the sofa in the den, soaking in caffeine, a vision pops into my head. I see Mother sitting on the porch of a beautiful plantation-type home overlooking a gorgeous garden. There is a path leading to the front porch. Mother is rocking with and talking with her mother and my daddy. Suddenly, Wade and Bob Anders, and Kirven and Marian Soloman (members of Mother and Daddy's Bridge Club) walk down the path to the porch. Mother looks up excitedly and exclaims, "Oh, there you are! We must get a bridge game set up for the afternoon. I have not played in so long."

I give in to laughter on the sofa. I relay my thoughts to Martha to not have her think me crazed. I do not know what the afterlife will be like, but in my mind, the glimpse of Mother sitting on the porch of the beautiful plantation home is the reality of my preconceived notion of a life hereafter.

Sue comes around 10 a.m., and she and Martha begin their duties as my 'spiritual servants'. I make phone calls to my friends and Mother's friends while they are busy in the kitchen.

I dress and prepare to meet Allen and John at the Funeral Home at 11 a.m. I take the obituary I wrote last week with me so John can read it and give it his stamp of approval. I found a small picture of Mother—the best in my determination ever taken of her—and will ask that it be used. She did not want her picture in the paper as part of her obituary. This will be the only wish of my mother's that I do not fulfill.

The beauty of her picture to me needs to be shared. It depicts the face of my mother the way she would want people to remember her. I feel I owe her—and I guess selfishly myself—this last visual remembrance. At the funeral home, we go over the details of the cremation—as that was Mother's wish. We set the time of her Celebration of Life Service for Thursday evening at 7 p.m. It will be held at her church. Now comes the time for the private family burial.

The time offered to us, due to the time needed for cremation, is Friday morning. John says that this time will not work for him as he is planning to go out of town Friday morning. I sit in disbelief over the conversation. My thoughts are, "What do you mean you have planned to go out of town? Are you aware that your Mother died last night and your life now goes on hold for two to three days?"

The anger inside of me wells up, but I cannot release it. It is not the time. Allen takes control and tells John that we will schedule Mother's burial on Friday morning and he can do whatever he wants to do after it is over. We settle on Friday at 11:30 a.m. despite the controversy.

We then have to identify the body. I remember this part of the pre-paid arrangements I made last summer. I remember being told that because Mother would not be embalmed her skin would be cold from the refrigeration and would be supple. I had wondered how I would deal with this. But, at this moment, I just want to see her again. I want to touch her and say my goodbyes one last time.

Allen, John, and I all go to the viewing room. Mother's body is laid on a small table draped with a pink sheet. She could not have appeared more beautiful to me. John looks at Mother, backs out of the room, and leaves Allen and me standing there.

I touch Mother's cheeks, kiss her forehead, and run my fingers through her silver hair one last time. "I love you, Mother" are my only words. Tears stream down my cheeks as I realize I will never be able to touch my mother again. How hard it is to give up the tangible even though you know intellectually that the body is only a temporary housing. Our soul is our self, but the body represents that self even after death. Pictures are wonderful, but the touch of a human being is forever lost. I turn to leave, look back at Mother, and say, "I love you" one last time.

From the funeral home, John and I meet at Newcastle Memorial Gardens cemetery. We make the arrangements with a representative for Mother's burial. Her urn will be placed in the plot beside Daddy's, and her name will be added to the same marker. I ask, for my future information, that if I am cremated also, can my urn one day be buried in the same plot as Mother's? The answer is, "Yes," but I will have to pay a right of burial fee today to do that in the future.

The right of burial fee is half of the current price of the burial plot. This is insane and nothing but a money-making racket!

But I end up doing this for my future. The representative then tries to sell me a pre-paid burial package for myself. I stop him in mid-sentence and say, "We are here today to make final plans for our mother. Stop trying to sell us stuff unless it is needed for our mother."

After three attempts, the representative gives up. John and I settle our plans with him, go out to identify the plot, and then go our separate ways. I ask John before he leaves when he and his family are coming to the house as visitation is in his mother's home—our home—my home. He says that he does not know.

I go home and spend the day greeting people and looking at the overwhelming amount of food that keeps pouring into this house. Carolyn, Josh, and Kelly come for about an hour in the early afternoon. John never comes. Neither does our extended family. Word has it that they are too emotionally upset over Mother's death. Gee, has anybody yet determined that I am too?

My long day comes to an end at 11 p.m. I fall into bed, but cannot sleep. Tomorrow I will need the strength to be with people all day and prepare for Mother's Celebration of Life service.

"God give me the strength to get through this before I fall apart!" Those are my only thoughts as I close my eyes, open my eyes, close my eyes throughout the night.

Thursday, June 13, 1996

I stay in bed until 7:30 a.m. I get up, make coffee, and stay in my pajamas. I am absolutely exhausted at this point. The culmination of the last few years on my body has taken its toll. But, for today, I must stand tall and endure.

Martha arrives shortly after 8 a.m. God bless her! She is truly Christianity in action. I shower and dress around 9 a.m. While I shower, I began to think about my brother and his family. By the time I am dressed, I am livid.

Throughout this ordeal, I have virtually been left by myself to take care of everything. They have no earthly idea what had to be done on a daily basis for Mother. And now she is gone, and where are they?

I decide that I have to call and speak my mind. Carolyn answers the telephone. John is not home. I began by saying that I am sorry she is going to have to take the brunt of this, but that I have to get it off my chest. I ask her if John plans to come to the house to greet people with me. Carolyn says that she does not know where he is, that he left to clean his businesses.

I semi blow up! I say, "Does he know that his mother died and the visitation is at her home—which happens to be my home. What am I supposed to tell people when they ask where John and his family are?"

Carolyn proceeds to explain to me how John does not handle things like this very well. She says that she is surprised that he was able to spend as much time as he did that last week of Mother's life at the nursing home. Carolyn tells me that when people ask where they are to just try and explain this to them.

I said, "Well, what I have been saying is that I don't have any idea where he is," and that is what I will continue to say." I simply hang up the phone at this point.

Do John and his family think this is easy for me? My God in heaven, can they not see that I am about to fall apart completely? And yet, I know I cannot do this until today and tomorrow are over. What is wrong with people who say they love you and yet run the other way? All the questions in the midst of grief are not healthy, and I realize that I just need to move on with what I must do today.

Martha, Sue, and I continue receiving friends throughout the day. The day goes by slowly for me. I have many sinking spells. I need rest, but cannot abandon those who come by. Guess it helps to have a family?

Around 6 p.m., I go to dress for Mother's service. A good friend has volunteered to come and stay at the house while I go. I am dressed and ready. I get to the kitchen door and stop myself abruptly. I happen to remember lipstick. Mother's pet peeve with me was the fact that I rarely wore lipstick.

I begin to laugh at myself. I retrace my steps to my bathroom. I cannot even find one tube of lipstick that is mine, but I do find a tube of Mother's. I take the cap off and discover that it is hardened from the *lack of use. I take my nail file and sand it down until I come to some creamy substance. As I apply it to my lips, I look up, chuckle, and say, "Yes, Mother, I remembered to wear lipstick."*

Oh, the tiny things that make all the difference. I am now ready. Mother's sister, Georgia, has come by the house, and I ride to the church with her and her family. It is good to see all of them and to have the opportunity to talk with them.

We gather in Allen's office at the church. What a nice-looking family we have, and what a tribute to Mother to have them all here. I talk with everyone except John. For some strange reason, he avoids me, and I find myself not even wanting to be near him.

At the appointed time, we leave Allen's office and proceed to the narthex of our church. When Allen opens the doors to the sanctuary, I have to stifle a laugh. Mother had always said that we might as well have her funeral in a funeral home because there would not be anyone there. The sanctuary is filled!

We file to the front as the congregation sings, "Joyful, Joyful, We Adore Thee." I truly feel a sense of joy and an ability to celebrate the life of my mother who has given me more than anyone could possibly ever know. She gave me, ultimately, the gift of unconditional love from the day she and Daddy adopted me until her last breath. I feel surrounded by that love and thus am able to deliver her eulogy as promised.

Read now the words of tribute given to celebrate the life of my beautiful mother. And remember that many of the words of this eulogy were from the Celebration of Life service for the lady instrumental in finding me and giving me to my mother and daddy for adoption. From the beginning to the end, love has now come full circle.

Mary Ann Russell Howie

In Memoriam
June 11, 1996

God chose an angel from above,
An angel sweet a fair;
He placed a halo 'round her head
To match her silver hair;
He gathered sunbeams for her smile,
From out the sky above;
He carved a heart of solid gold
Then sprinkled it with love;
He picked the stars from out the sky
To give her eyes of blue;
He gave her courage, hope, and faith,
To last her whole life through.
God chose an angel from above,
So sweet and fair to see.
He called her Mother and He gave
This angel fair to me.

—Author Unknown

IN MOMENTS LIKE THESE, WE WALK SOFTLY and speak in hushed tones, for this is a tender time. But it is not a time of tragedy. Indeed, there is something very beautiful about the home going of one who has lived such a long and useful life, so crowded with devotion to the noblest causes which evoke our human loyalty and commitment.

Mary Ann Howie lived for the noblest and the best in life. She lived for her faith, her family, and her friends. Life is full of mystery, and it brings many questions which elude our human answers. What shapes a life to make it great or small? Why do the righteous suffer? Why do the wicked seem to prosper? On such matters, philosophers and theologians will disagree; skeptics and believers will disagree. But on one point, theologians and philosophers, skeptics and believers are all agreed: Life is what you make it.

Some come into the world as favored recipients of fortune's bounty, laden with the gifts of Providence—yet they make a shamble of life. There are others who come into life without such favored gifts; they walk a road marked by hardship and tragedy—yet they make of life a symphony of beauty and meaning. They take what life offers and weave a tapestry of faith. Mary Ann Howie was one of those.

We will not dwell on her problems, for all of us who gather in this place are familiar with the burdens which she bore. But she never asked, "Why did this happen to me?" To have asked this question would have violated two cardinal principles of her life. In the first place, to have asked that question would have meant whining in the face of difficulty, and this she never did. Complaint was not her nature. She was a believer and an optimist. Courage is the word which epitomizes her life, and no soldier on the battlefield ever had more of it than she. It was a courage born of faith. Her faith kept her, but she did not keep her faith to herself. She shared it with all whose lives she touched. To have asked that question would also have meant doubting the unfailing goodness of God. And, this she never did. Undaunted and never discouraged, she believed in the goodness of God. The words of Sydney Lanier most appropriately describe her faith.

As the marsh-hen secretly builds on the watery sod,

Behold I will build me a nest on the greatness of God:

I will fly in the greatness of God as the marsh-hen flies

In the freedom that fills all the space 'twixt the marsh and the skies:

By so many roots as the marsh grass sends in the sod

I will heartily lay hold on the greatness of God.

And it was in that greatness of God that Mary Ann saw life as a blessing and a privilege. To watch her children and grandchildren become adults was a joy, and knowing she was a great-grandmother was the ultimate happiness. Mary Ann believed that there was only one great adventure ahead of her, the greatest experience of all, the only perfect happenstance in life—with no strings attached, no loose ends—absolute perfection. That was death viewed as the perfect ending to a long, happy life with the knowledge that in the goodness of God she was born, in the Providence of God she was kept all through her life, and in the love of God a place was prepared for her in Heaven which she viewed as a garden where she would again find those dear ones—family and friends—who made her world.

Benediction

Eternal God, our Father, we thank Thee for life, and all that makes life sweet and worth living.

We thank Thee for the pleasant world Thou have given us to live in and the good comrades who share our life together by ties of blood and the bonds of friendship.

We thank Thee for great friends who have come to strengthen our spirits, to enlarge our vision, and to gentle our souls.

We thank Thee that so many human hearts are so kind and love lights more fires than hate can extinguish and that our world grows better as the earth grows old.

It is good to be alive, and we thank Thee for the joy of living.

We thank Thee, too, for death. These bodies of ours were not made to last forever. They grow tired and worn. And we thank Thee that when our work is done, and the day is spent, we may turn homeward to live with Thee—free from all the limitations and weaknesses of the body.

We thank Thee that our times are in Thy hands not our own, and that we have not the ordering of our lives, but live and move in Thee, whose wisdom is love and whose love is wisdom.

We thank Thee that every one of us is of concern to Thee, and that Thou hast a stake in us; that Thou has given us work to do and dost add our hearts and minds to the working capital of Thy Providence.

We thank Thee that Thou dost not let us live in vain if we live our best.

We thank thee now for Mary Ann whose life on earth has come to its final chapter with Heaven opening to a time of high promotion and coronation. May her life continue to be an inspiration and a guide to us in the future. May we ever do Mary Ann honor by being more like her, and may we show our love by doing the things she loved best and by being the kind of men and women in whom she always took pride.

And let us believe as Mary Ann did, that "in everything God works for good with those who love him," so, "in all things we are more than conquerors through him who loves us," being sure that "neither death, nor life, nor angels, nor principalities, nor things present, nor things to come, nor powers, nor height, nor depth, nor anything else in all creation will be able to separate us from the love of God in Christ Jesus our Lord."

We give back to nature only that which is natural, for this is all that the grave can hold. To Thee, Father of us all, we give back a radiant, glowing, child-like spirit. In the remembrance that Mary Ann was so much in love with life, we can imagine how she has now burst into that larger and fuller life of Heaven. Grant unto her a triumphant and joyous entrance into the eternal kingdom. Let the trumpets of welcome sound, and the voices of angel choirs, cherubim, and seraphim, sing praise to the living God. In the Savior's name, we pray. Amen.

Following the service, I just walked out the door of our church and returned to the house. John, his family, and our extended family stayed to greet people. I could not stand with them at this point. Our house was soon filled with family and friends. John and his family came after the service. They stayed in one room, and I stayed in another. After most of the people were gone, I went to the room where they were and pretended to talk with them. I did not know what to say to any of them at that point. It was 9:30 p.m. before all was quiet on the home front again. I finally went to bed around 11 p.m.

Friday, June 14, 1996

This morning, I will go to Newcastle Memorial Gardens for a private family burial for my mother. I am up early and by myself for the first time in many days. I sit drinking coffee and reflecting on the storm which I have braved. So much of it right now seems like a dream, and yet it stabs through my heart still.

I will dress in a little while and complete Mother's long journey home for her. Around 10a.m. Allen comes to get me and we go to Newcastle Memorial Gardens. A small portion of the family has come, and we enjoy talking with each other until all have arrived.

We take our respective seats, and Allen proceeds with a short, sweet service of parting for Mother. We conclude with a prayer of thanksgiving for her life and for all she has meant to all of us. I have time now to talk with all who have come to share this last leg in Mother's journey. The love she gave to so many is so evident in this place. Family was important to her, and she loved so deeply. Her gentle ways have been passed on to each of us.

Mother never got to see her great-grandson, David. We decided to take a picture of Georgia (Mother's sister) holding him. Somehow this completes yet another part of her journey. I can tell that Will is having a hard time with the cremation part of this day. I will talk with him later and explain that not only was this his grandmother's wish, but I feel that it is a beautiful way to visualize her release from the horrors inflicted on her earthly body and mind. Our time is short here. Allen takes me home. As I was getting out the car, he said, "May I ask you a question?" "Sure," I replied. Allen asked me how I had gone through the death of Howard, my friends going back to Texas, and the death of my mother and was still able to smile and find good in life? I simply replied, "Perhaps if I had not had all the love and joy Howard, Dave, and Donna brought to my life, I would not have been able to make it through. That loved filled my heart to total capacity and enabled me to experience the joy in the journey as I walked my mother home with grit and grace through Alzheimer's. Allen hugged me and left. I spent the rest of today by myself—mostly sleeping from exhaustion.

A New Beginning

June 14, 1996

FROM HER HUMBLE BEGINNINGS IN A SMALL TOWN to a small room at Meadow Brook in that same small town, Mother's long journey home was complete. It was time for me to begin walking through my own journey.

I had so much debris to clean up from the storm that raged through my life as I completed Mother's journey with her. Alzheimer's fragments not only the person with the disease but also those closest to it. It is like pieces of a jigsaw puzzle thrown on a table. Each piece is a part of the big picture but must be turned the correct direction to join other pieces to complete the puzzle.

I found myself consumed with nursing home issues, estate issues, family issues, church issues, and my personal issues as I tried to begin walking *my* journey. All these pieces of my puzzle needed my attention.

In times like these, people search for an immediate ending to their storms. I realized early on in my new journey that there would not be an immediate ending. A friend said to me during this time, that perhaps "there is no ending, but simply a New Beginning." That struck me profoundly. So, it is that after the rain, I began to piece together my new beginning in what turned out to be a prolonged and painstaking journey lasting twenty-two years.

June 1996 to October 11, 1996

It has been four months today since Mother died. So much has happened. I have completed many home projects which have helped to occupy my mind during this time.

I have been proactive in making positive changes at Meadow Brook. I have requested a copy of Mother"s records from Meadow Brook and have begun researching a Medicaid Fraud issue. I am consumed at this point in an attempt to rectify wrongs for all persons who are living their last days wrapped up in an illness that leaves them speechless

I am successful in filing a Medicare Fraud claim at the State level. A representative from the State Judicial Office came to meet with me, and I turned over copies of all documents related to my claim to him. He explained that the results of this claim may take several years as a thorough investigation will be on-going from this point forward.

I feel peace within as I pursue righting this wrong that affects so many people in nursing homes; where they have lost their voice, someone needs to become that voice for them.

I still visit some of the great friends I made at Meadow Brook to continue being a part of their lives and to minister to them. I find peace each time I return there. "It was the best of times, it was the worst of times," but in the end, I know that I have come away from this experience holding on to the "best of times," always remembering the moments of joy in the journey as I have begun to move forward with my new beginning.

I have met with Mother's attorney several times to bring closure to her estate. The bottom line is that there is no estate. What little funds Mother had accumulated were spent for her care. Bills keep coming in week by week. Mother's attorney sends me a formal letter acknowledging her funds are depleted and her estate is closed.

I have received numerous bills from Queens Clinic and have been turned over to a collection agency for medical charges dated after Mother's death. On October 1st, after numerous calls to them, I go to the Clinic. I sit before a billing representative and ask for specific dates and services for these charges. She begins telling me that they were for doctor visits for Mary Ann at Meadow Brook all dated after June 11, 1996.

Apparently, Mother was seen one to two times weekly by one of their physicians. I looked at the billing representative and said, "I am not responsible for these charges, but I need to tell you face to face that Mother died on June 11th. I don't mean any disrespect to you, but if you can tell me how and where Mother was seen on these dates, I would love to know so I could visit with her again."

The billing representative, at this point, was in total shock. I ask her to remove the charges and to mark Mother's file as closed. She states that she could not do that as the computer system will not allow her to do that. I tell her I felt like a simple click of the delete button should work fine. The billing representative looks at me and says, "But you are her Power of Attorney." I reply that I was her Power of Attorney, but the law states that at the moment of someone's death, that the Power of Attorney ceases.

Perhaps I am somewhat rude at this point, but somehow I need to get my point across to this Clinic. I look at the billing representative and simply say, "I am leaving you a copy of Mother's Death Certificate. Any future harassment of me by Queens Clinic for fraudulent bills will be turned over to Mother's attorney."

I thank her for her time, stand up, and walk out of her office and return home. I chuckle all the way home and, at the same time, wonder how many people this happens to, and they just pay the bills.

Two other medical practices and Kingsbury Ambulance Service continue to hound me, also, to the point of my being turned over yet again to a collection agency. I send everything to Mother's attorney as I choose not to fight this on my own. And, with this, I have closure.

To find some reconciliation with my church, I talk with Allen numerous times. I ask him if I could do a month-long seminar on Wednesday nights in October to tell my story and give valuable information to others who are walking, or may someday walk, the road of Alzheimer's with a loved one or a friend.

Allen feels that this is a great idea. The title of my seminar is "The Grit and Grace of Elder Care."

The first Wednesday in October, I tell Mother's story—my story—mostly to increase the awareness of victims of this disease and the awareness of the needs of caregivers. But also, I tell our story, hoping my church will come to realize the neglect it displayed in ministering to Mother and me during this time. I remain extremely bitter and want this to help me as I deal with the bitterness—and to help members of my church realize the effect of neglect of any family facing this crisis.

The second Wednesday, I have the social worker from Meadow Brook come and talk about the ins and outs of nursing home placement, finances, and involvement of families in all persons' lives that are in need of their services.

The third Wednesday, I have Mother's attorney come and speak about financial planning before the fact to not deplete family funds. He also has information regarding Wills, Power of Attorney papers, and Health Care Power of Attorney papers.

The last Wednesday, I begin by asking the question, "What does this church do to minister to families in crisis such as Mother and I experienced?" Several members stand up and talk about the wonderful ministry by the church when a member dies. I just stand and look at each one of them in disbelief! Sure, our church ministers beautifully in times of death, but what I want to know is what is done during the crisis leading up to death?

My anger toward my church took over at this point. I turn to Allen and ask him to come to the podium to take my place. I am shaking from head to foot. I want to scream out at every one of them and ask, "Why? Why did you do nothing for Mother or me? Do you not understand the devastation I felt and still feel as a result of your actions/lack of

*action in our lives for the past four years or more?
Why did you let us go through this alone? Did/do
we not mean anything to you?"*

*My deacon's wife, Sue, seated in the back of the
room, stands up and states what I cannot say. She
admonishes members of our church for their neglect in
a reverent, beautiful way, a way I am not capable of at
that moment. I will forever be grateful for Sue and her
courage to help our church understand their actions.*

*There is little discussion from this point on, and
I walk out of the room and go home. I realize that
forgiveness and closure to the hurt I feel inside
toward my church is extremely far away at this
time. I know, at this point, that I will not be going
back to my church. It hurts too deeply. I grew up
in this church—was very active in this church.
So was my mother until the year before she died.
Because of this church, my brother became an
ordained minister.*

*I am not able to find any understanding of this
loss in my life now. I realize that it is going to take
more than a few months to begin to know how to
bring closure to this issue in my life to make a new
beginning, and I also come to the realization that
sometimes to bring closure and find peace, you
have to move away from the hurt. Perhaps this is a
piece of the puzzle that will not find a place in my
new beginning.*

November 1, 1996, to November 30, 1996

The most significant thing about these last four months is that only once has my family called me and that was to get the name of a contractor. I cannot fathom that not only did they not support Mother and me through these last few years, not only did they not come and be with me when Mother died, but they do not know if I am dead or alive now.

Families are supposed to love and care for one another through good times and through not so good times. I feel abandoned, and I guess I am.

I know I have to give up the hope of sharing with them since all the indications given to me are that they have nothing to share with me. Over these last few years, their lives did not change due to Mother's circumstances. They had each other, and their lives went on. Maybe they did not realize what it was like to be totally responsible for the care for Mother. They certainly do not understand what it is like to be alone. You cannot force people to care and express their love and concern for you. But how do you forgive your family for turning their backs on you and on Mother when we needed them most?

I cannot go on letting my anger toward them destroy what is left of my world. The hurt predicted by Mother is so real. I look at her picture often

and say, "I know that you said this would happen, Mother, but I did not realize that it would be this hard."

This must be the loneliest walk in the world, but I plug on, hoping that somehow I will continue to grow through it, accept that I am alone, and learn how to meet life head on, no matter what it brings.

I pray that God will guide me so I may continue to fulfill my chosen mission. I pray that the angels will somehow let Mother know that I try to keep the smile of her love alive daily. It is not easy. I understand so well the emptiness she lived with for many years after my daddy died. But at least she had me.

Perhaps the months ahead will be kind. Maybe they won't. Whatever they bring, I will muster the strength Mother taught me to have and do the very best I can each day. And when I go to bed each night, I will pray to God to forgive my shortcomings and that He will hold me tightly in His arms until I, too, complete my journey home one day. There are times I would like that journey to end today, but I think I still have much to do. I will keep on keeping on.

All Saints Sunday at our church is November 3rd. I have called my family and asked them to come with me to this special service to honor Mother. They, as usual, have an excuse not to come. I talked with Will who has just started a new job out of town and invite him to come. He loved his grandmother so much! He came and spent the weekend with me and went with me to the service to honor her. What a loving and caring young man he is. We shed tears, but most of all we shared love with each other. Before he left me on this beautiful day, he told me, "I would not have been anywhere else today but sharing this time with you honoring Grandmother!"

Later that same afternoon, I am going through pictures and find the one made last Thanksgiving with Mother at Meadow Brook. I realize again that the only people touching anyone else in that picture are Will and me. He has his arm around me, and I have one arm around him and my other hand on Mother's shoulder. Everyone else is either just standing or have a hand on Mother's wheelchair. What a powerful statement of reality from our last Thanksgiving together that continues one year later. Most times a picture is worth a thousand words.

I also have thought I feel I have told my church goodbye today. There really isn't anything there for me anymore. It is a very sad ending to a long relationship. Yes, the closing of another door. But sometimes to forgive something/someone, you have to leave them. I hope that a door will open for me in the future to be a part of another church—a church that puts their doctrine into practice for all people. In the meantime, I hope God understands my attending All Saints Tabernacle (a name I gave to the quiet meditation time I experience on Sunday mornings in my own home).

Time marches on. The holidays are not something to which I normally look forward. I am not giving Christmas presents this year. Financially, I cannot spend the money, and in my heart, I do not have the energy to focus it.

I have found myself $40,000 in debt for expenses I paid for Mother's care. I found out too late that part of this was not my responsibility. I did not have any guidance for this period of time and spent whatever was needed for her to have good care.

I will begin to dig myself out of debt this year. Perhaps not giving Christmas gifts this year will turn out to be a good thing. Perhaps it will lead me on a more peaceful meaning of what Thanksgiving and Christmas are all about.

I do not look forward to being alone, but I will manage. My good friend, Sheila, will be home for both holidays. She and her mother got me through last year, and I am sure will help me through this year. But it will be hard. At least last year I was still able to share Christmas with Mother—and I was able to share Mother with our family one last time through meaningful gifts.

The strength is there for me. Mother taught me well. Life has taught me well. And somehow I will find it and hold tightly to it, and out of these experiences, I will grow and find meaningful lessons that will enrich my life.

There is a beautiful article in our newspaper today. The Saturday before Thanksgiving each year, The Pilot Club of Charlotte sponsors a Lovelight Celebration at Freedom Park here in our city. Luminaries are placed and lit all around the lake in memory and honor of special people. All the money made from this event goes to Alzheimer's Research. Wow! I send in a donation in honor of special people in my life, in memory of so many who have gone before, and in celebration of the life of my beautiful mother! I write a letter and mail it to my family and friends. I include a copy of that letter here to give special meaning to this celebration. I feel so good inside that this extraordinary celebration fell into my lap and that there is a reason for thanksgiving in my life. Sometimes I feel God speaking to me in mysterious ways. This is one of those times.

Love Light Celebration Letter to Family & Friends
November 23, 1996

My dearest family and friends,

The holiday season is here. All over town, decorations are appearing. The malls are stocked with merchandise for us to buy for those special people in our lives. Christmas shows, holiday musical programs, and church services are advertised throughout our city. Office parties and gatherings in the homes of friends are being scheduled at a fast pace with calendars being filled to capacity already. All of this and much more signal the beginning of the most beautiful season of our year.

For me, I have chosen a simpler route that I want to share with you in the hope that you will share a part of it with me.

On Saturday, November 23, 1996, luminaries will be placed around the lake at Freedom Park in honor or memory of loved ones. One of those luminaries will be for Mother. Other luminaries will be placed as I honor family and special friends. I plan to go and take a walk around the lake to celebrate her life and to celebrate the beginning of the holiday season in the true spirit of giving.

I hope that many of you will join me
in this celebration. Also, in that same
spirit, I plan to decorate an angel tree at
Meadow Brook. This I will do very soon
after Thanksgiving. Some of you know that
I still visit my friends there—people who
are residents and the staff. This has been a
comforting experience for me as I share in
the lives of those who need an affirmation
of love and in those lives that give that
affirmation of love daily.

I feel blessed that so many loved and shared
with Mother and me in the time that she
lived at Meadow Brook. A note I found after
Mother's death, which I have shared with
many of you, has prompted this different
form of celebration: "Give a smile to someone
who is sad or to those who don't expect one;
joy for any occasion, especially when you feel
my presence. Put your arms around someone.
Give to them what you want to give to me. Let
me live in your smile, your joy, and in your
love. At every opportunity, share me."

This, my family and friends, is true
Thanksgiving and the Spirit of Christmas.
I invite any of you who can to participate in
these activities with me. The Celebration
at Freedom Park will begin at five o'clock.
The angel tree will be decorated Sunday

afternoon, December 1, 1996. If you would like to participate in either event, please call 725-5416, and we will plan accordingly.

In the Spirit of the legacy of love that Mother gave to us all—faith, family, and friends—my wish for each of you is a holiday season filled with the warmth of sunshine, laughter, and most especially love.

November 17, 1996, to November 30, 1996

Each day this week, I have come home from work hoping to have a message from my family that they plan to join me in the Lovelight Celebration. Alas, there have been none. I do not understand why they choose to ignore this. It is also almost Thanksgiving, and there has been no word of a family get-together that we usually have on Thanksgiving Day. Waiting, always waiting.

Saturday comes. This day is hard for me. No word from my family about tonight and their coming to celebrate Mother's life with me. I pick up Martha at 5 p.m., and we go to the park. My lifelong friend, Joyce Deaton, Allen, Peggy, and Bill and their son and his wife, Sue and Chet, Sheila and Lynn are there to share this special night with me. What a beautiful experience.

There were close to two thousand luminaries placed around the lake. There was also a full moon shining brightly. We walked about three-quarters of the way around the lake before we found Mother's luminary. The light shining there was brilliant. Seeing her name on her luminary brought tears to my eyes. I held on to Allen for a few moments allowing my tears to fall. They were tears of celebration for her life and tears of resignation that my family had once again deserted me. I wish that they had cared enough to share this special moment with me.

I know that Mother's spirit shines brightly still in my heart, and I hope that I can continue to fulfill the legacy of love that she gave to me throughout my life. To miss that would have been a tragedy for me. I guess that is why I cannot understand not even receiving a telephone call from my family.

I had dinner with Martha and Gary at their home. After dinner, I drove back to the park by myself. I sit in my car and listen to beautiful dulcimer music, looking at the majestic lights. I pray to God to take away my anger and give me the courage to give up that which is not mine any longer. It hurts. I cry all the way home.

On Monday, I talk with my Administrator at school. December 10th will be my last day of work for this year. I will go back on January 6th. I am physically and mentally exhausted and need some time to reflect and to rest. I plan to spend some time at Meadow Brook with my friends. I plan to do some cleaning. I plan to curl up one day and just read a book. I need to relax.

I am not sleeping well. I must come to some resolution about my family. I keep telling myself to give it up and go on with life, but that is easier said than done. I wish they would communicate with me in some form or fashion and tell me why they obviously no longer consider me family. Families should be about love. Behind love is always action. I am not whining and saying "woe is me." I just need to know what direction I should go in from this point on to understand how to forgive and move on through life.

I search daily for answers. I continue to pray to God to take away my anger and help me heal and go on with what it is I am supposed to be doing here on this Earth. What I do know is that there are people who care and little children who need my love so desperately. Perhaps this is what it is all about. I need to get through the holidays and move forward.

Saturday, November 30, 1996

The last day of school was Wednesday. I waited all week to hear from my family, but no response. Each day and evening, I hoped that there would be a phone call, but none came. I resist the urge to call them, even to the point of not being able to sleep and having crying spells. It all began last September.

The end of September, I called my family. I talked with Carolyn. Somewhere in the conversation about how much she had to do, she mentioned going to have Kelly's wedding dress fitted. I said, "What wedding dress?" And, that is how I found out Kelly was getting married November 30th.

At that time, I had planned to go out of town for Thanksgiving. I told Carolyn that and said that I wished that someone had told me earlier. Oh well, what can I say? As the days flew on, I decided not to go out of town. I just decided to stay home for Kelly's wedding. At the beginning of November, Carolyn called wanting the addresses of our family. I gave those to her. No one questioned whether I would be here or not. And so the story goes.

I did not hear anything from them about Thanksgiving Day. I went with my good friend, Sheila, and her mother to have Thanksgiving lunch with her grandmother and her aunts. It was a delightful meal shared with a family, but it was not my family.

I came home early afternoon and cried until I could not cry anymore. My heart is absolutely broken in two. I cannot believe that my own family did not make contact with me for this special day, especially the first Thanksgiving without Mother! I just do not understand and probably will never understand. How can you totally abandon your sister and not care whether she has anyone with whom to share Thanksgiving?

This is not a petty oversight. It is not being too busy with the wedding. It's breaking the heart and spirit of someone you supposedly love and who is your family. How can human beings be so cruel? I do not know, and today as I write, I do not want to know. I am sure that the response would be, "Why did you not call us?" Well, in the five months since Mother's death, that is exactly what I have been doing, but you have only called me three times, and that was to ask for the telephone numbers of other people.

This time is different. I cannot call and beg to be accepted. My heart and spirit will not let me do that. The family was there, and if they did not want me to be a part of their day, I could not go and ruin it for them. And that is the way it is. But let me tell you that I am one broken spirit.

As I sit at my desk this morning and look at our Thanksgiving picture taken with Mother last year at Meadow Brook, I grieve—not for her—although I miss her terribly. I know she is with God, and the host of heavenly angels, and her family. I grieve for my family that seemingly is no more. Oh, they have each other, but they certainly have made it clear that they do not want me. This is a greater loss than losing my mother.

Thanksgiving night, I cry until my eyes are swollen shut. As I try to sleep, I think that maybe the years ahead will be kind, and I can grow to accept being alone. This is what time, the marvelous healer, does for us. But I do not think my heart will ever mend from this experience. I ask God to take away my anger and bitterness, but the brokenness is something that will not heal quickly—if ever.

I call Kelly this morning—just to tell her that I love her, and I would see her this afternoon. I want to be there for her on her wedding day, but I dread seeing John and Carolyn. I cannot help but feel this way. I am not even sure they want me to be there. I did receive an invitation in the mail after my talk with Carolyn but have had no personal contact with either of them. I guess there was a rehearsal dinner—but I do not know. I did not receive a card to return to let them know I would be in attendance, and I know from talking with other members of my family that cards were sent to them.

I love Kelly so much and am so happy for her on this day. None of this is her fault, and I will be there for her. When the wedding is over, I plan to leave and let them celebrate the way they have chosen. I will not interfere where I am not wanted. Perhaps I judge too harshly, but what else can I think? Besides, Sheila and her mom have invited me to go to a local fish camp with them when I get home from Kelly's wedding.

I arrive at the church at 3:30 p.m. It is raining, and I did not know how traffic would be, so I left home a little early. I was sitting in my car when John came down the walk. I blew my horn, and he saw me. He came to my car. When I opened the car door, I began to cry. We hugged each other and told each other that we loved each other. He made a remark about my car and said that he just had to make it through the wedding. I brushed the hair back from the back of his jacket. We went to the church doors.

When they opened, Will was standing there and immediately hugged me. Carolyn was a few feet away from me, and the expression on her face was one of shock.

I signed the register and went to see Kelly. She was so beautiful. When I came out of the little room, Carolyn was talking with her sister who was directing the wedding, asking, "Where will we seat her?" Will simply took my arm and immediately took me to the family row. I sat a long time by myself. Carolyn's family joined me later.

The wedding was beautiful. Jeff cried when he saw his Kelly. She was such a beautiful bride!

Each time I made eye contact with John, I nearly lost it. I just kept saying to myself, "Fish camp, fish camp" over and over, as I was going out to dinner with Sheila and her mother. That helped me keep my composure.

When the ceremony was over, I walked down the aisle to the back of the church. Carolyn's sister hugged me and told me that everyone was so happy I decided to come. Why was everybody shocked I was there? Didn't they understand that this was the only place I would have been and it would have been nice to be included rather than to be made to feel like a stranger?

Oh well, I go to my car and begin crying hysterically. I cry all the way home. When I reach my home and start to pull into the driveway, what to my wondering eyes should appear? There were two huge pink flamingos in my yard!

I stopped the car halfway up the drive and began to laugh. No one ever confessed to having put them there. Whoever came while I was at the wedding was an angel in my life. I desperately needed comic relief at that moment!

I go into the house, change clothes, go to the fish camp with Sheila and her mother, and have a joyous evening!

The important thing about this day is that I did go to Kelly's wedding and share that precious moment in time with her. I hope that someday it will mean something to her, I hope that there are angels of which we are unaware in our lives always—angels who put pink flamingos in our yards when we need them most!

December 1, 1996, to December 31, 1996
December 6, 1996

It is a week after Kelly's wedding. Carolyn calls me this morning. She wants to know if I am okay and asks why I did not come to the wedding reception. I merely say that I just couldn't. In trying to say even that to her, my voice cracked. Some things are just better left unsaid at this point. After all, it has been made perfectly clear that understanding my feelings and where I am with my life right now just does not matter to them. Bottom line, I did not get an invitation to the reception.

If you have not walked in the shoes of someone else, I guess you really cannot understand their circumstances. Carolyn did say that I should share Christmas with them, that having little David was going to make this Christmas a happy one for all of us, and we just would not think about Mom and all the bad stuff. We would just have fun.

I shuddered to hear that. Yes, it will be fun with the baby. I will go and share with them. But I feel that the experience will probably be like sharing Christmas with strangers. I know nothing about their lives for they have completely shut me out. But they are my family, and if I hear from them as to when they would like me to come, I will go. But, nothing can keep me from thinking about Mother!

The bad stuff is not what I dwell on. I honor her by keeping her alive in my memory. At this season, I think about all the wonderful times we shared together through the years and how fortunate I was to have such a loving and beautiful Mother. That will always live in me. True, life goes on, but it is also true that it is good to talk about those who have meant so much to us, and especially to talk about them with family. I guess we are all so different, and I just cannot understand. That, I am sure, I will have to deal with in time.

Tuesday, December 10, 1996

Today is my last day of work until January 6th. I am taking time off for myself as I am physically and emotionally exhausted and hope that some time away will help. I often go to Meadow Brook and spend time with my special friends. I take goodies to the staff who were so wonderful to Mother.

Wednesday, December 11, 1996

Ever needed a fun time in your life? I sure do need one right now. After the sun has set on this day, a friend and I go to Allen's home and tie pink flamingos that have red garland around their necks in the huge oak tree at the front of his home. We repeat this at Sheila's home, too. I laugh so hard that I cannot keep my eyes dry. Oh, to see their faces when they get up in the morning and see their new Christmas decoration! What great jocularity—and how badly I needed it!

Saturday, December 14, 1996

These days off have been wonderful! I have basically done little, and today I am sick. I have a call in to my doctor and am waiting to see if they will call in medication in for me. What a bummer!

Yesterday, I told Allen I would not be participating in our church Tableau with him. I just do not want to do it—just can't do it.

Sheila is coming back home for Christmas holiday this week. We are going out to dinner with another friend. With Sheila here, it will be one adventure after another. And right now I need adventure!

December 31, 1996

Today is the last day of 1996, and it seems only right to enter my thoughts into my journal after being absent for a while.

The holiday season brings to mind the opening lines from A Tale of Two Cities: "These were the worst of times—these were the best of times." Just as my journey with and through Alzheimer's Disease was.

Emotions are high with ups and downs all along the way, but this is to be expected with this being my first Christmas without Mother. The emptiness and being alone are devastating. Except for a few good friends, the feeling of abandonment is at an all-time high. I struggle to understand these feelings and to understand what continues to contribute to these feelings. They are real.

Through the years, friends who have been close just do not call or make an attempt to contact me anymore. Perhaps it is time to close some doors and move on to others. Maybe this New Year will allow me to do that.

Sheila and her family continue to make me a part of their lives and a part of their family. At their home there are gifts under the tree for me, a stocking is hung on their mantle for me, and their love fills my heart always. They are all a beautiful expression of what life is all about. We had so much fun together Christmas Eve and again on Christmas morning. We were family.

My worst hurt continues to come from my own family. I did receive a call from John on Christmas Eve. When I returned home from Sheila's house, there was a message on the answering machine from him. He invited me to come to his house for Christmas Day.

I went to his home on Christmas morning after I left Sheila's. Carolyn and I had a wonderful talk, and I am glad that I went. I am very concerned about John as I feel that he is suffering from depression and running away from life right now, but unless he makes time for me, I will not be able to talk with him about it.

He slept almost the entire time I was at his home. Sharing Christmas with the rest of the family was great! It helped to begin to heal some wounds, and it did make Christmas Day a good one for me. What a beautiful experience to hold David and see his smile. Love is there, and I must find a way to be part of that love in the future. They need me as much as I need them.

I invite and share a special time with Sheila and her mom at my home to end this Christmas day. I prepare a meal for us and find pleasure serving that meal at my table again. The table has been bare too long. Sharing with friends in your home is so special, and I know that during this next year that I must get back to doing this.

Most of all during this time, I just miss Mother. I go to Meadow Brook and share with those who need me there. I am glad that Mother is not suffering anymore and wish that she was still here, but at the same time, I know that I would not bring her back like she was for any reason. It is such a huge bag of mixed emotions. I have felt her so strongly in my life throughout the holiday season. Seeing a reflection of an angel from her watch that I am wearing while driving in the city is not imagined. It is real. I let it remind me of all the good in life that she taught me and know I must share this with others the rest of my life.

Throughout the season I am reminded of a quote from the movie Shawshank Redemption: "You either have to get on with living or get on with dying." It is time for me to get on with living, carrying all the good of Mother in me and giving of good to others. That is a life well lived—to make the most of each day and forget the shortcomings perceived in others. Do that which is right in my life and live the legacy Mother left to me.

I miss most Mother's affirmation of love on a daily basis. I miss her touch, her hugs, and her "I love you" expressed to me every day. I still hear her sweet small voice at times deep in my heart.

As I begin 1997, I will try harder to be the special person Mother knew me to be—not perfect, mind you—but trying my best every day to give unconditional love and care to others, just as the Keeper of us all gives to our lives continually. That is my wish for this New Year, and that is the legacy I will strive to live each day. Just "Thank you, Mother, for all of your life and for the meaning it has for my life forever. I love you!"

So, how do I spend New Year's Eve, the last night of 1996? I will be at home. I have invited Sheila and her mother for dinner. We will grill steaks, fix enormous salads, baked potatoes and load them with butter and sour cream, fix Southern sweet tea, and open a bottle of wine after dinner for toasting in the New Year!

My home was always a home filled with people sharing with each other, and I will bring back that home tonight. It feels good.

I was shopping this afternoon and bought a Runestone, which is an ancient stone of prophecy. It is the stone of protection. It signifies optimism, defense, protection, and represents positive human striving towards the Divine. This is the tone I hope to follow for 1997.

I have made no resolutions as such, but positive human striving toward the Divine lived out in my everyday life is a challenge I will take on in this next year. Beyond that, I do not know what the year will hold.

This year—the year Mother completed her long journey home—completes a long journey for me, too. The lessons I learned along the way are the ones which shall guide my path in the coming year. I pray to God that I will do His will for my life and that my life can be an inspiration to others.

I always ponder why I am here. I hope that the simple act of living out my days will signify at least to humanity the reason.

Protect my paths.

Oh God, guide my feet

and continue to carry me when I need to be carried.

Forgive my shortcomings.

Be ever present in my life.

Always be a reflection through my life that others see.

Turn my heart toward forgiveness of my church and my family.

Grant me peace in the days of 1997.

January to April 1997

January is here, and it is back to work. It has been good to have time away to gain a little strength both physically and emotionally. I move on into this New Year continuing to seek restoration of my own life. I go to work, come home, prepare for the next day, go to bed, and ease into a rather mundane lifestyle.

I pour all my energy into my work and keeping up the house. There is still an emptiness inside me that I have not been able to fill since Mother's death. This emptiness still fills me from the loss of my church and my family in my life. I ponder how to deal with these things and get on with living, but ponder as I might, I also know that this will continue to be a long road.

January 14, 1997

Today is my birthday. Martha and Gary sent a beautiful flower arrangement to my school for me. How special they both are in my life! They are taking me out to dinner tonight to help me celebrate.

Since I have not heard from my family, I look forward to sharing this day with them. Just before I am leaving school to come home, I am paged to take a telephone call. It is from John. He asks me if I would like to come and have dinner with them. I tell him that since I had heard nothing from them, I have already accepted an invitation for a special birthday dinner celebration.

I am glad John made the effort to invite me to his home for dinner, but why, oh why, did he wait until the last minute. It just seems to me that I am a "last minute thing" in their lives always.

I go to dinner with Martha and Gary, share a beautiful evening, lots of good laughs, lots of love.

Back at home, I just cry. The one thing lacking on this day in my life was a true affirmation of love, the kind that Mother always gave me. It is so hard to live without the physical reminder of love in your life. You can fill your days with work and chores at home, but the emptiness you find when you walk through the door of your home each day is sometimes unbearable.

All the things you do in life just seem to have no significance if they are not shared with someone you love. I still cannot believe the sense of abandonment that I feel in my life. It is real and continues to be a hurtful wound.

I think about my church. I was there last October for the Seminar I gave on the Grit and Grace of Elder Care. I was there in November for All Saints Sunday. I have not been back since. And no one cares. The message from the church that I receive is I mean nothing to them.

It is clearly time to move on. I need to go back to a church, and I will, in time. I am just still too emotionally fragile now and cannot make myself get up and go. I think a part of me just cannot accept any more hurt from a church, and my heart is afraid.

I pray God will lead me back and help me find a group of Christian people who care and who would share with me on my journey. This is such an important aspect of life.

So it is that my first birthday without Mother has come and gone. There will be more to come and, hopefully, in the years that follow, they will be celebrations of the love that has filled my heart for all these many years rather than spent pondering an empty heart.

February 1997

This is the month of Mother's birthday and will not be an easy one emotionally for me. Her birthdays were always so special and celebrated grandly, but I will move forward through it because I must.

February 17, 1997

This day comes and goes leaving me with only a heavy heart and a river of tears. Once again, alone. No one in my family remembers that today is Mother's birthday, or if they do, they do not acknowledge it with me.

I am beginning to have a feeling that I need to distance myself from Meadow Brook for a while. Just seems to make me sad each time I go and each time I leave. Perhaps I need to close that chapter in my life and find a new one to open. Close a door, open a new one. Close a door, open a new one. Perhaps, that is a part of what life is all about. Maybe it is all of what life is about.

I feel a little less anger toward my church as I have separated myself from it. Now do not get me wrong, I have not forgiven my church for its abandonment of Mother and me, but I have found a degree of peace in the acceptance of that abandonment by closing that door in my life. It creaks open every so often, and I pray that one day true forgiveness will come from me for them, and I can close and lock that door without the fear of it ever resurfacing.

My anger toward my family continues. They have not called me since my birthday. There is no acceptance regarding this hurt in my life. I do not know how I will ever be able to forgive them.

Ah, puzzle pieces yet to placed as life continues day by day. Maybe the greatest question left unanswered is, "Do these puzzle pieces even have a place in my puzzle? Do they have a place in my new beginning?"

March 1997

March comes and goes without any change in my life. March 22nd is the most special day in my life each year. It is the day I was adopted! It is better than my birthday. It's better than any day. This is the first "Nancy Day" that no one celebrates but me. Wow! More than an emotional drop on this day.

The realization has set in that there is no one who will ever care about this day again in my life but me. That is more than tough.

My cousin, Peggy, happens to call me the evening of March 22nd. She asks how I am doing and I begin to spill my guts to her. She was never aware of this date in my life each year. Oh, she knew I was adopted, just never knew the date.

It was good to talk to someone about this and about so many other things, especially to be able to talk with someone about my mother! She loved my mother—she just leads a very different life than I do and does not have much time to give. I am just grateful for her call and the impact I hope it will have on my life in the future.

April 1997

With April comes the celebration of 'John Day,' the day John was adopted. I know the hurt I felt in March when my 'Nancy Day' was ignored, and I sit down and write him a letter and send him a small gift to celebrate his day. I share it with you here.

Dearest John,

There really is not an appropriate card for this day. Yes, I guess in its own right, it is a birthday, and for many years we celebrated it as one. Those were good years—full of love from a mother and daddy who loved you dearly.

You were a choice for them, and I guess to me that is what makes adoption so very special. I think that we were both very fortunate and God certainly had a hand in all the work. To have grown up in such a loving and giving family is to be cherished all of one's life. And no greater love could have been given to you—or to me.

Although we do not have many opportunities to express love to each other, I hope you do realize how much I do love you. And even if no one else realizes how special today is—I do! Without this day, I would not have had you for a brother.

I read an article in the paper recently about adoption. The ending of the article quoted, "To love a child is to touch the face of God." I think that was the way Mother and Daddy felt about you all through your life. Through you, God brought them many blessings, and they could touch His face daily.

Today they are in His Presence and for this a part of us rejoices. And then there is the part of us that will always miss their love and touch. Mother called you one of "God's greatest treasures." She was right!

Anyway, through all this rambling, in case no one else knows how special this day is, Happy John Day! It is not only special, it is important!

April 17, 1997

Just four weeks ago, I went to the hospital with severe chest pain.

Three weeks ago, I asked John to come over so that I could talk with him. I wanted to give him a copy of my Living Will and talk with him about my upcoming medical tests.

Two weeks ago, I called him and asked him to come by school so that I could give him copies of some more legal papers. I tell him I find myself not able to comprehend how he could let me go through all of this and not give a damn whether I was dead or alive. Why does he shut me out completely? I am sure if I were a member of his church, he would be right by my side!

When you are by yourself and your family makes the decision to totally ignore your existence on the face of the Earth, you do wonder at times what there is to live for. I wish John and his family could know and fully understand what it means to be alone in this world. They have each other through good times and through not so good times. I know that their lives are busy, but it seems to me that a phone call does not take five minutes of your time, and yet it can mean the world to someone else.

I have wanted to call them all day, but I am not

going to. A part of me wants to see how long it will take them to find out if I still exist. It is so hard to let go and, even though I know that would be the best thing to do for me now, I just can't. I will work through this somehow—but I don't think the hurt will ever go away.

We were brought up and taught to love one another. I thought we did, but now I wonder how superficial that love must have been. My mother and daddy loved me and showed that love daily. I have had such love for forty-nine years and now feel the emptiness where love once grew.

If love is not expressed, if care is not expressed by those closest to you, what else is there? Maybe there is nothing left to say. The coming weeks are going to be hard for me with the ending of another school year and the anniversary of Mother's death. Probably no one will feel it as intensely as I will, and I seriously doubt that anyone will express whatever feelings they have to me. I am just glad on this day that Mother and Daddy instilled in me the fact that with God you are never alone.

The thought crossed my mind that the hymn, "Never Alone," was the first one I memorized and learned to play on the piano. I guess it might have been an omen from the beginning. I pray that God will grant unto me understanding and allow my heart to forgive, even if it might mean closing that door sometime in the future. I have tried to keep it open, but this event is making it speak louder and clearer to me. Perhaps one of these days, I will just stop trying. Perhaps I should just pray, "Dear Lord and Father of mankind, forgive my foolish ways."

THE FIRST ANNIVERSARY

June 11, 1997

It is the last day of school and the anniversary of Mother's death. This has been a hard week for me as the memories of a year past stay at the forefront of my mind.

John called me Monday, but I was not at home. We play telephone tag until Tuesday evening. When he called, I must admit I was shocked. When he calls back on Tuesday evening, he talks in his usual generalities. He did ask when I would finish up work. I tell him that Wednesday will be my last day of school for this year. He asks what I will do then. I tell him when I leave work on Wednesday I plan to go by the cemetery. I ask him if he would like to go with me. As usual, he cannot go but will try to get by and see me on Saturday. For some strange reason, Saturday never comes this week.

I leave work on Wednesday and go to the grocery store. I buy the biggest most beautiful red rose that I can find. I drive to the cemetery and lay it on Mother's grave. My tears fall on the headstone like rain. I say a prayer of thanksgiving for Mother's life and for what her life has meant to mine. I cry in anguish as to why I suffer alone. I have no answers and probably never will.

My friend, Suzanne, is the only person who acknowledges this important anniversary in my life. I will always be grateful to her for all the love she gave to Mother and to me and for all the support she gave to my life as I walked with Mother on her long journey home. I guess there is no one else on the face of this earth that it meant anything to. That is the sad part. To have lived the beautiful life that you did, Mother, and to be forgotten by everyone in one short year is beyond my comprehension. Some people suffer and are ministered to by others who feel their pain and walk with them. Others are left to only hold on to the hand of God and walk their road alone. I do not know why, but I feel the pain of being alone in all of my life. I am not lonely—I am just alone.

It would be good to have someone to share you with, Mother. The deep roots of family that you worked so very hard to build are lost to me, and

I really think that I will never have them again. It hurts. I will press on in trying to understand and to let go of that which I cannot change.

Today, I feel that it is not worth the fight. Tomorrow I may feel differently and hope that I do. Today it would just be good to lie down to sleep and not awake to the turmoil that rages within.

Just know, Mother, that I love you and remain grateful for the impact you have had on my life. You gave me so many beautiful gifts from your heart, but the greatest gift of all is the ability to love and care for people in everyday life. That gift is both beautiful and tragic at the same time. For it is that gift of not being with me by anyone in my family that continues to cause me the most pain. You knew that pain, and yet you continued living with a smile for all you met. I will try, and I must do the same!

Sitting in the sunroom later in the evening, I am gazing into the clouds with loving thoughts about Mother and the beautiful life we shared. In the clouds—as clear as clear can be—I see her face as it is depicted in the beautiful photo I have of her in the den. It stops and seems to hover over my home. I look away, and when I look back, it is still there.

I hear her voice saying to me that everything is going to be okay; that I am going to be okay. She tells me that she will always be with me in my heart and will still be holding my hand through all circumstances of life. She tells me to hold fast to her hand and to the hand of God in all things. Then she says, "I have to go now. I love you with all of my heart."

Her face fades from the clouds, and my tears fall. Not really sure where this gift came from; I only know that I will carry it with me throughout my life! It does not matter if anyone ever believes this story. For, you see, it was real to me!

The First Anniversary—perhaps the hardest. I hope so.

The First Year—also, perhaps the hardest. I hope so.

EPILOGUE

Living with the Gifts . . . Finding Joy in the Journey

AFTER THE FIRST YEAR OF MY NEW BEGINNING, I came to the realization that the years of riding the world's biggest, scariest, fastest emotional roller coaster through my walk with Mother and Alzheimer's still had left pieces of my puzzle scattered all over my table. These puzzle pieces, most likely, would never be able to be turned the right way to fit the puzzle of my new beginning.

Why?

They can't be, for my new beginning is not part of that same puzzle. Oh, there will always be fragments of those pieces that will live deep in my heart forever, but my new beginning is mine and mine alone. Now I must walk my own journey with the courage, strength, resilience, blessed hope, and love without end that those fragments brought into my life.

I must continue searching deep from where I am, move forward, and live life with the gifts that the joy of the journey has given to me—the gift of the knowledge that the journey through Alzheimer's with Mother molded me for greater good; that it was both beautiful and crooked and as it should be; that it took every moment of every situation of that journey to bring me to the presence of now; and that now is the right time to begin to celebrate the joy of the journey.

2018

THE YEARS HAVE COME AND GONE, and my life has been through many changes through them. These changes have brought growth to every aspect of my life and to my new beginning. In the background of each change, there have always been the gifts of life Mother gave to me through all our years together. Her gifts of faith, strength, wisdom, laughter, tears, guidance, acceptance, discipline when I needed it, hugs, her message of grace and always hope, her believing in me, and, most important, her gift of unconditional love. For all these and so much more I find that my gratitude is to the Keeper of us all for giving me love without end through her. For, you see, through my mother, I witnessed the voice of God and the hand of God in my life every day

My life through the years of my new beginning, even though filled with change, and even though sometimes not easy, could not have been more abundant than to have lived in God's grace and in His loving care through continuation of the blessings, the continuation of the joy from the journey walking with Mother brought to my life that will remain in my heart always.

When taking the first steps of my new beginning, I acknowledged to myself that living through Alzheimer's with Mother brought more pain to my life than I ever thought imaginable, but it also brought untold blessings I was not able to see while walking that journey with her.

Looking back while moving forward gave me the realization that through that walk my life was given endurance that I would not have thought possible. My life was given strength and courage that I would never have thought possible. My life was given the opportunity to give my mother the love and the care that she had always given to me. My life was given a brave new understanding of death as peace. My life was given the opportunity to walk the walk, not just talk the talk of true unconditional love as an outpouring from my soul to all those who would continue to walk with me through all the days of my new beginning. My life was given the ability to minister to those who would find themselves walking in the shoes of Alzheimer's, or through any disease.

The depths of despair I encountered through Alzheimer's brought wholeness to my life that I would not have had if I had not walked this journey with my mother. Alzheimer's softened my soul and created a gentleness of heart I otherwise may have never known. It brought the gifts of redemption, forgiveness, and peace to my soul. It brought the knowledge that even in the worst times of your life when you need people the most, you can accept the fact that some will not be there; you will need to accept that you will walk many miles on your journey alone. The gift of acceptance of those times will allow you to continue walking without becoming hardened to your world. Without acceptance, you will have lost the joy in the journey.

Looking back, through and beyond the pain of the disease, I realize that the heart of my mother continues to beat within my heart as her beautiful life continues to be a constant guide and always will be through and beyond my new beginning. Sometimes I put my hand over my heart and feel and hear two hearts now beating as one. I acknowledge the pain, but I am able to move forward with the blessings of these two hearts guiding my path, and I feel the joy in the journey!

To claim this joy, I realize that I need to have all the blessings my mother's life gave to mine and all the gifts that walking hand in hand with her through Alzheimer's gave to me.

Close at hand, is an old knapsack that I mentally fill with every gift and blessing received throughout my life and through my journey with Mother. Along my new pathway, I always keep that old knapsack nearby. No matter the circumstances that my pathways take, I have only to reach into my old knapsack and take hold of the blessings and gifts I need to keep on keeping on.

My new journey has brought many changes to my life as I have continued to walk forward carrying my knapsack of those gifts given to me through my mother while walking with her, hand in hand, heart to heart.. Those gifts have been the cornerstone of my journey. I have stopped at the many pathways I have traveled on the journey, paused, and unpacked the gifts I need to continue walking on. The beautiful thing about the gifts is that they never run out. They are always there filling my knapsack and always available to me. The willingness to use them throughout life is the key to finding joy in the journey.

My first new pathway found me re-reading my journal that I kept through the devastation of Alzheimer's in Mother's life and mine. I realized as I recalled the events so clearly that I needed to write a book, the book I wished I could have found when I walked the journey; a book that might serve as an inspiration and a guide to help others feel some peace as they trudge forward moment to moment, day to day coping with the pain.

Mother always wanted me to be a writer. How ironic it would be that our journey through Alzheimer's would become the book she always wanted me to write and through the writing of it the ultimate joy could be given to others.

So, I began to write. I relived all the moments, all the days, all the months, and all the years. There were times when it became too painful to keep writing, but I felt determined to tell Mother's story, my story, our story. As I continued writing, I realized that within Mother's journey, within my journey, there were the journeys of my brother, the journey of my family, the journey of my church, the journey of friends, the journey of disease— literally journeys upon journeys that brought loss, but also brought gain to my new beginning. All these journeys, all the losses, all the gains would become a part of my new beginning. If I gave myself time and space to pause and use the gifts in my knapsack, all these journeys would become an everlasting gift that would fill my heart with joy in every circumstance of my life.

My new beginning began when I decided to sell the dream house I had purchased for Mother. To do this, I relied on so many gifts in my knapsack to carry me through. I bought a small condo close to the same neighborhood and began a new life that helped me tremendously to downsize the debt I encountered through Mother's care and gave me the blessing of my own small home where I could continue my journey. In this move, I found peace and joy surrounding me each moment of each day.

My next pause along the path caused me to rely on multiple gifts in my knapsack. I had major back surgery, and for the first time in my life, I faced disease without the comfort of my mother's arms surrounding me.

Following the surgery, my neurosurgeon explained to me that a former fusion had broken loose and if I had made one wrong move, I would have been paralyzed from my waist down for the rest of my life. These words find me to this day thanking God each morning when my feet hit the floor. I recovered nicely from that with the help of Chet and Sue Helt who took me into their home for a short period rather than have me go home alone. This was the first hurdle. It was hard. It was lonely. I clung to all the gifts in my backpack and through it all found joy. Most of all, I found it in walking! And walk onward, I did.

I paused again on my path to pursue the dream of finding my birth mother. It was not very hard to do. Through great detective work on the part of Sheila, her mother, and me, we located a copy of my Birth Certificate at the Courthouse in Albemarle, North Carolina. The only problem was that we had no way to prove it really was me. I contacted a reputable agency which specialized in adoption, and within twenty-four hours they called me. Yes! The Birth Certificate we had located was indeed mine. My birth mother was no longer living, but the agency was able to contact a birth cousin who agreed to talk with me!

I will never forget the day I met her. She invited me to her home. I took pictures of me growing up with Mother, Daddy, and John. She shared stories with me about my birth mother and her life. My birth mother took me to my birth cousin's home from the hospital. There were already four other children in that household, and they could not afford another child.

My birth mother kept me for nine weeks. She nurtured me, fed me, held me, loved me, and then she gave me a gift of the most unconditional love a mother could ever give to her child. She gave me up for adoption knowing she could not give me the life she wanted me to have.

She went on to marry years later. She had a son who developed Crohn's Disease and died. She then lost her husband. My birth mother never got over giving me up for adoption and, after the death of her son and husband, she became an alcoholic and died at the age of 42.

I now have pictures of her, and when I look at her photo, it always brings a smile to my heart. I know she loved me! Each Mother's Day, I celebrate the lives of both of my mothers. Through this experience, my circle of life was complete, and I once again found joy in the journey.

To walk the pathway set before me, I would need so many of the gifts and blessings from my old knapsack. This path had been so steep and rocky and seemed as if it were an insurmountable mountain to climb, but with strength, grit, grace, courage, and hope, I knew that I must go forward.

It was nine years after Mother's death that my family called and invited me to go on their family beach trip. I grabbed handfuls of gifts and blessings from my knapsack to be able to cast aside all the baggage I had carried with me through the years and try and discover where I truly belonged as a member of this family.

I saw this as a chance to renew relationships and try and draw closer to each of them. At the coast, it felt good to share laughter, fun, hugs, movies until midnight, walks on the beach, sand in our shoes, coastal sunsets, and sunrises that brought renewal to my life.

John and I got up each morning to have coffee and watch the sunrise over the ocean. It was so peaceful being with him in this beautiful place. We talked and talked and talked each morning.

One morning, he turned to me and asked, "Nance, was there ever a time that I hurt Mother or you because I did not have time for you?"

My eyes welled up with tears as I said, "Yes."

With that door open, I began to pour out my heart to him over the hurt of his absence through Mother's years with Alzheimer's. I emptied my heart into his on that morning, and he emptied his into mine. His only question was, "Can you ever forgive me?"

That morning, with the rising sun over the ocean, God led us both to redemption, forgiveness, and peace. That morning we came back into each other's lives as brother and sister. A bond was formed for us both that lasted all the days of his life. It was a bond that allowed us to fully experience the unconditional love God gives to us in our lives through each other. It was on this day that I began to realize that even though things would never be perfect with my family, I loved them and would always be there for them. Yes, at the

Coast, on that deck, with that sunrise, I found the peace of forgiveness that has allowed me to move onward down the pathways of my journey with gratitude for all that was, all that is, all that will be, and all that may not be.

Yes, that sunrise at the Coast, casting its rays down on John and me, gave to both of our lives the gift of redemption and forgiveness that allowed us both to see the joy in the journey. It took so many of the gifts and blessings from my old knapsack to move through this experience, but oh, those were multiplied a hundred times over with the gifts and blessings received! I truly left the Coast with a much larger knapsack after that trip for I now had the love of my family tucked tenderly inside my heart. And inside my heart, it would remain for all the days of my life. Little did we know at the time, on that day, how much the power of the gifts given and received would be needed in all of our lives later. The pathways I walked led me into retirement, a total knee replacement, and through a heart attack. Each of these experiences claimed their own set of gifts and blessings from my knapsack.

Being able to retire after forty years of teaching was exciting, to say the least. A whole new world opened to me and life was filled with joy! I soon learned I needed a knee replacement, found an excellent doctor, had the surgery, went through the rehabilitation, and was restored to good health.

The gifts and blessings from my old knapsack carried me through this with strength, courage, and hope.

Soon after my full recovery, out of the blue one fine day, I suffered a heart attack. I was taken to the hospital by a dear friend with my only symptom being that my whole jaw hurt so bad! Forty-five minutes after reaching the Emergency Room, I had surgery, a stent placed in my heart, and was resting in Cardiac ICU.

Two days later, I was home. It took a long time to get over the fear of having another heart attack. It was a pathway of my journey when I had a hard time as I longed for Mother to be near me, to hold my hand, to wipe away my tears, to calm my fears. I often reached my hand into my old knapsack to grab hold of the blessings and gifts Mother had given to me, and at the same time would put my hand over my heart and feel her near me, guiding me, and inspiring me to keep on keeping on.

Mother's gifts and the blessings of the journey we walked together once again renewed me and enabled me to experience the joy of being alive and able to continue my new journey.

My new beginning now brought me to two pathways I did not want to walk. John had retired and come home from West Virginia. He was so happy to be back and had a never-ending To-Do list to help his family. Then suddenly cancer reared its ugly head in his body again, and he began his fight for life.

He told me one day as I brought him home from a chemo treatment that there really was something good about cancer and it was the time that it gave us to be together! I thought back to that sunrise at the Coast that brought us forgiveness and redemption and reunited us as brother and sister. I can only thank God for that day as it enabled me to minister to him through his cancer, to hold his hand gently as I had our Mother's hand, and walk him home when the time came with unconditional love.

Had it not been for my walk with Mother, I am not sure I could have walked that road with John with so much grit, grace, and dignity. And, believe you me, it took every blessing and every gift in my old knapsack to walk with him and accept his death as peace.

Then right slap-dab in the middle of his fight, I was diagnosed with cancer! When I went to tell John about my diagnosis, he gently took my hand and asked me when my treatments would be completed. I told him. He told me that morning that he would be with me all the way and promised me to be here with me to celebrate the end of my treatments. And he was. We celebrated from his hospital room with a smile on both of our faces and so much love in our hearts for each other.

Even fighting the battle of his life, a battle he would not win, John was my great encourager through it all. He will always be my hero of the faith! There just was no greater love! There was no greater joy in the journey than entered my heart on that day. I will always thank God for sunrises at the Coast for they are forgiving and redeeming blessings given freely to our lives that enable us to experience unconditional love through the hearts of those we love.

I have continued having to accept many losses in my life.

The loss of people in my life going through cancer was and remains huge. Never in a million years did I think those closest to me would disappear in the times I needed them most. But for various reasons and reasons I cannot fathom, they did.

I have survived cancer now for three years. The drugs to survive this disease took most of the reserves I had saved for those rainy days in life and for fun vacations away. I probably will never get my medical expenses paid off and probably will never have a comfortable nest egg again. That I must accept and learn a new lifestyle.

I do not feel I can get close to people again as the hurt from losing them is just too much. So, I will live with my feelings inside of me, accepting that my definition of true friends just did not work out in my life; that it must be easier to say I love you, rather than show it in actions; that many times you cannot rely on people to be there for you. My life was changed forever by cancer, by loss, and the side-effects of the very drugs that saved my life left behind.

Gone were the happy-go-lucky days and the focus had to be on surviving and living with pain, a focus that has taught me to just show up in life and do the best I can to live the best life possible, continuing giving to others regardless of what they do not give to me.

Somehow, through the physical and emotional pain, I am finding a way to experience joy again within myself without having to rely on others to bring it to me. I have pulled many gifts and blessings out of my old knapsack to help me. I have found that the gift of acceptance is the only way out and into a new life of joy through loss.

I would be the first to say it is easier said than done. The gift of acceptance has allowed me to move through the grief of the loss of people I have loved with all my heart. I have moved through the loss of my church in my life. I have moved past the loss of my family I felt through the devastation of Alzheimer's and into the acceptance and realization that part of the devastation of the disease is that it has a way of separating and dividing love, bringing pain and loss temporarily to families. The acceptance of this has led me to believe with all my heart that the bond of love given to us by our awesome God can never be destroyed! I have come to the acceptance that life goes on and love never dies. Through these everlasting bonds, there is joy in the journey with your family that will follow you all the days of your life!

FULFILLING MY DREAM

The Gift of Joy in the Journey

THE GIFT OF UNCONDITIONAL LOVE GIVEN TO MY LIFE through all the gifts of the journey became the driving force in my life. Through this, I now unpack from my old knapsack all the gifts from my journey through Alzheimer's and pursue my final dream of that journey: publishing my writings to help others.

I find myself deep into the editing process with the hope of publication in 2018. There is my joy. There is the new life in my new beginning! My hope is that *Joy in the Journey* may be an inspiration to someone who is faced with walking with and through a long journey home with a loved one. It is devastating to all, but oh the blessings it can bring to life when in the end you realize that the voice of God and the hand of God were with you all along; that you were never alone; even through all the times you felt like you were.

It is my hope for anyone who will ever find themselves reading my story, my mother's story, the story of walking together on her long journey home—that on the other side of that journey you will see and feel the beautiful truth that it was a gift to your life! It was a gift that will alter your life through all your days and give you the ability to lead your life with ultimate gentleness, grit, grace, strength, courage, hope, redemption, acceptance, and forgiveness. It was a gift that will keep on giving to your life, in your life, and through your life, all the days of your life that will bring you peace in your own new beginning—a new beginning where two hearts beat as one bringing joy and inspiration that will guide you through all the days of your life. It was and will be forever more be a gift to your life from the Keeper of us all who has the power to fill your heart on a moment to moment basis with joy in your journey!

Through the receiving of that joy into your heart, you will now be able to give your joy into the hearts of others who need you in their life. Because of the gifts from finding joy in the journey, your new beginning will now lead you into a joyful, triumphant song of life.

—Nancy Elizabeth Howie

ADDENDUM

Planning a Peaceful Path
Walking the Long Journey Home with a Loved One

If you have not already, you will one day walk with a parent or loved one on their long journey home. As with any journey in our lives, advance preparation provides a more peaceful path for all involved. The greatest need is to plan: a "What-If Plan." This needs to include the parent or loved one and all family members. Discussions need to take place, and a consensus needs to be reached well in advance by all participants. None of us know what tomorrow may bring to our lives. But, with a plan, no matter what comes, we can be ready to meet the journey head on with confidence, grit, and grace.

Family Meetings

Hold a family meeting with your parent/parents or loved one and discuss your "What-If Plan" with them: finances, legal documents that need to be in place, medical decisions that they may face, community care arrangements if the time comes that care inside or outside of the home is needed, caregiving options, and end of life planning. These are not easy discussions to have for many, but they should take place well in advance.

Legal and Financial Issues

Legal and financial advice needs to be obtained along with asking the advice of a Financial Planner. Seek an attorney who specializes in Elder Care, as they know specific laws that govern legal issues for this population.

Everyone needs a Will—a current Will along with a Durable Power of Attorney. These are documents that can be prepared well in advance of their need, but that will make the "What-If" journey a much easier one for all concerned.

Be aware of Insurance, Medicare, and Medicaid Laws that govern the finances of your parent or loved one and that will help cover the expense of care when needed.

Living Trusts and other financial trusts can be set up to protect the finances of your parent or loved one. Research and get advice on investing in a Long-Term Care Insurance Policy for your parent or loved one. We all work hard for our money. We all work toward investing in our future. So, seek the legal advice needed to protect those investments of your parent or loved one.

Medical Decisions

Medical decisions may have to be made along the journey. It is essential to have your parent or loved one make those decisions well before they are needed and while they can make them on their own in their best interest. The ultimate decision for their medical needs is theirs. Help your parent or loved one complete a Health Care Power of Attorney and Advance Directives that will cover medical decisions that might need to be made for them. When the time comes that these decisions need to be acted on, it is a comfort to know you are carrying out their wishes rather than having to make those decisions for them during an incredibly emotional time in both of your lives. Make sure these papers are filed with their doctor's office, your hospital of choice, the State, and that copies are kept in a safe place with your family.

Community Care Services

SERVICES IN MOST COMMUNITIES FOR CARE VARY from homemaker services, home health aids, adult daycare, assisted living facilities and nursing home care. Research what is available in your community and the cost of each well before it is needed. If the time comes that your parent or loved one needs assisted living or nursing home care, it is much easier to have discussed this beforehand.

It is always good to visit these places in your own hometown as a time to gather information. Many assisted living facilities and nursing homes offer tours and an opportunity to talk with someone about the facility and pre-planning. Take advantage of these opportunities with your parent or loved one before an emergency arises and a crisis finds you scrambling to find something affordable and suitable for your parent or loved one.

Become knowledgeable in knowing regulations for short-term and long-term nursing home care, Medicare, and alternative payment options available. Advanced planning for all these can make your journey a smooth one rather than one over an unknown rocky road.

If your parent or loved one needs nursing home care, be an active participant in their care daily. Keep records daily. Question their care, their medications, their diet, their activities, all on a regular basis. Get to know the Director of the nursing home, the social worker, the nurses, the CNAs, the doctor who services the nursing home, the therapists who work with your parent or loved one, and families of other residents, etc.

Be present each day—at different times of day or night—to be able to see the care your parent or loved one is receiving. You don't place a parent or a loved one in a nursing home to relieve yourself from the responsibility of their care. You place them there because physically and or mentally they need that care. You need to remain an active part of it, just in another environment.

End of Life Decisions

THESE ARE PERHAPS SOME OF THE HARDEST DISCUSSIONS you will ever have with a parent or a loved one. Not one of us wants to lose someone we love, but this discussion is very important. It should include cremation or burial decisions, what funeral home to use for services, what services they want from the specified funeral home, where the burial will take place, and where the Celebration of Life service will be held if you choose to have one, and who and what you wish to have included in the service. If you have taken the time to make these decisions with your parent or loved one, when the time comes that they are needed, you will know that you followed their wishes and their Celebration of Life Service was carried out the way they wanted it. And perhaps they will be smiling down on you and saying, "Thank You!"

Caregiving

Seek advice from agencies in your community involving care giving for your parent or loved one. Caregiving is a full-time job and demands a grit and grace you never gave a thought to until it is needed. Plan with your family. Plan with your church members. Plan with your friends. Know how you will deal with the demands of caring for your parent or loved one as you walk with them. Take advantage of any and all available help along the way.

Take Care of You

TAKE CARE OF YOUR OWN PHYSICAL AND EMOTIONAL NEEDS throughout the journey. This is very important. Seek help from every source you can find that will support you along the way. It is a long and winding road and can be extremely difficult. Do not feel guilty about asking for help. Get connected with agencies in your community. Set personal health goals such as eating a healthy diet and getting a good night's sleep. See your doctor. Tell them that you are a caregiver and do not ever hesitate to mention any concerns you have.

Be kind to yourself. Do the very best you can. Provide the care your parent or loved one needs in whatever environment they find themselves. And, in the end, there will be no regrets. You will know you followed their wishes and did the very best you could to keep them safe and give them the care they needed. You will know that you walked with them on their long journey home with ultimate love. And no matter how rocky the road in your life, when you complete that journey with a parent or loved one, you will realize the blessings of that road. You will realize that it was a gift in your life, a gift that will live forever in your heart, a gift that will give you strength and courage for the walk of your own long journey home one day.

ACKNOWLEDGMENTS

I WOULD LIKE TO EXPRESS MY GRATITUDE to all who have enabled me to fulfill my life's dream of publishing *Joy in the Journey*.

To those who generously gave of their time to read my raw manuscript, who came to me when their reading was completed with their affirmation to me to "Get this out there to help all those who so desperately need it." And, all those who have walked with me hand in hand through every step of the publishing process.

To Jo Giles for her encouragement throughout this process which began with her helping me edit my raw manuscript, and who has walked with me believing in my ability to fulfill my dream.

To those close friends who generously volunteered their time to be beta readers for proof copies of *Joy In The Journey*: Coreen Button, Barbara Milford, and Jo Giles. Each of you in your own way have affirmed the value of this publication and my heart thanks you!

To Richard Paul Evans who through his book, *The Christmas Box*, gave me my first moments of *Joy in the Journey*.

His book fulfilled my Mother's last Christmas wish . . . as she gave Richard's book to family and close friends as her gift of healing, remembrance, and joy. And, for Richard's sponsorship of The Walk Cruise, that gave me, through his Personal Assistant, Diane Glad, the opportunity to meet, talk with, and give my raw manuscript to Karen Christoffersen.

To Karen Christoffersen, Director and Producer with BookWise Publishing in Riverton, Utah, for believing in me as an author, for the guidance and inspiration she has given me to complete this journey, for believing in *Joy in the Journey* and it's message for all those who need it. Her patience and kindness given to me through the publishing process has been extraordinary! Karen has been one of the greatest blessings given to my life and has proved to me dreams really can come true! Because of her, I now leave a legacy that will be an inspiration to others and will transcend time and space.

—Nancy Elizabeth Howie

ABOUT THE AUTHOR

Nancy grew up in Charlotte North Carolina. She currently resides in Pineville, North Carolina. Nancy graduated from Myers Park High School in 1966 and attended Appalachian State University where she received a Bachelor of Science degree and a Master of Arts degree in Special Education.

Nancy taught children with mental and physical disabilities for forty years. She began her career at the Mecklenburg County Center for Human Development. From there, she transferred to the Metro School and completed her years of teaching at Beverly Woods Elementary School in 2010.

Nancy believed that to teach children and be given the privilege of working closely with their families was to "touch the face of God" daily. Her career, while challenging, brought unconditional love to her life daily.

Nancy is an avid reader. She enjoys coastal visits to her beloved Sunset Beach that she claims to be her Heaven on

Earth, visits to the mountains of North Carolina, being at home with her four-legged companions, Russell and Kasay, her Shih Tzu "furever friends," long lunches with special friends, serving on the Board of Directors in her community for many years, and maintains a deep appreciation in the ability of music to bring joy and peace to her life.

Upon retiring, Nancy had one dream—complete a manuscript she had begun in 1997 detailing her walk with grit and grace through Alzheimer's Disease with her mother.

Nancy completed her manuscript, and at a Self-Publishing Workshop sponsored by #1 *New York Times* bestselling author, Richard Paul Evans on his *The Walk* Cruise, was able to talk with Karen Christoffersen, Director and Producer for BookWise Publishing and give her a copy of the manuscript. In September 2017, Karen came to Pineville, North Carolina to accept Nancy as one of her authors!

Joy in the Journey is Nancy's first literary work. It's the book she wished she could have found while walking with her mother through the daily devastation of Alzheimer's Disease. It is her wish that *Joy in the Journey* will be a blessing to those who find themselves walking with a loved one on this same journey . . . and that in the end, as Nancy did, they can see and feel the blessings that journey brought to their lives.